Growing Up Happy in a Lonely World

Nicole M. Morrison

LIVE DIFFERENTLY
PUBLISHING

GROWING UP
happy
IN A LONELY WORLD
A Mixtape Memoir

Nicole M. Morrison

LIVE DIFFERENTLY
PUBLISHING

Live Differently Publishing
Bismarck, ND

Growing Up Happy in a Lonely World

© 2026 Nicole M. Morrison

ISBN (Paperback): 979-8-9941587-0-8

Published by **Live Differently Publishing**
Bismarck, North Dakota
growinguphappybook.com

This is a work of creative nonfiction. This memoir is told as the author remembers it. Conversations and scenes have been shaped by memory and perspective, while remaining faithful to the truth of each experience.

Cover design by Nicole M. Morrison
Interior layout by Rachel Connolly

First Edition
10 9 8 7 6 5 4 3 2 1

DEDICATION

For Nicole,
who sees me and holds me with grace.

For my boys, Nick & Nate,
who gave me purpose
and taught me how to love with my whole heart.

For Scout,
who keeps me curious, present,
and wild enough to dance in the rain.

And most importantly—
for the younger me—brave, broken,
and quietly holding it all together.
I came back for you.

Vulnerability has never been in my vocabulary.

Contents

DISC ONE: Off the Record

DISC TWO:
Break the Silence

DISC THREE: Full Volume

OPENING NOTE: DON'T STOP BELIEVIN' (THE HEARTBEAT OF THIS BOOK)

This is not your typical memoir—
it's a mixtape of moments.
Some beautiful, some brutal,
some still unfinished
A rhythm of memory, healing, and becoming.

And like every good mixtape, it comes
with a soundtrack.

Music has always been how I stayed afloat.
When words failed,
songs like "Bring on the Rain," "Iris,"
and "Don't Stop Believin'"
held me together.

Long before playlists,
I'd sit by the radio with a blank cassette,
waiting for Casey Kasem's Top 40—
finger poised on the record button,
trying to capture the songs that said
what I couldn't yet put into words.
They said what I didn't know how to say.
They reminded me I wasn't alone.

If you've ever felt invisible,
mislabeled,
or like you had to shrink just to fit in—
this is for you.

These stories aren't polished.
They're real.
Told in broken-line rhythm
because that's how I lived them:
interrupted, aching, and eventually—
resonant.

You'll notice this book is structured like a 3-disc set:

Disc One: Off the Record – where silence and survival ruled.

Disc Two: Break the Silence – where questions cracked things open.

Disc Three: Full Volume – where I stopped asking for permission to be me.

Each track is a heartbeat.
A confession.
A scar turned into a song.

You will also find throughout this book,
playlists of songs–
Some that cracked me open,
Some that carried me forward,
And some that live in the back pocket of my heart.

And while the story is mine,
I wrote it for you.
The one still trying to make peace with your past.
The one who learned to smile while breaking.
The one who's ready to remember who you were
before the world told you otherwise.

You're not alone.
You're not too late.
And you don't have to carry it all quietly anymore.
This book is for anyone
who's ever had to fight to stay soft.

To stay open.

To stay.

So go ahead—
press play.
And whatever you do...
Don't stop believin'.

Opening Note Playlist

"Don't Stop Believin'"– Journey
"Secrets" – One Republic

Opening Note Reflection

What's the song that's carried you through?
Not the one you play at parties—
the one that knows your ache.
The one that held you when no one else knew how.

What would your mixtape sound like?
Not the highlight reel—
but the moments that cracked you, shaped you, saved you.

And what would happen

if you stopped shrinking
and let the full volume of your story rise?

This isn't just a book.
It's an invitation.
To remember.
To reclaim.
To press play on the parts of yourself you were told to skip.
What track in your story deserves to be played out loud?

ALL ACCESS

GROWING UP HAPPY IN
A LONELY WORLD

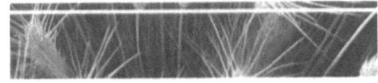

VIP PASS

Backstage Access Granted.

Scan the QR code above or go to **nmstrategy.com/ growinguphappy_vip**.

Enter password **SideBVIP**

Unlock exclusive access to:

- photos
- companion journal
- full playlist of songs mentioned throughout the book
- exclusive Side B moments

Preface

PREFACE: MY GIFT

When I was around seven,
my grandpa told me I had a gift.

Not the kind you wrap in shiny paper.
He said my voice was a gift.
He was not referring to a singing gift—trust me.
I never once thought I'd be the next Celine Dion.

Okay, I take that back.
"It's All Coming Back to Me Now."
There were a few legendary car rides with my sister
where we belted Celine's song
like we were prepping for a world tour.
The rearview mirror was our spotlight.
Windows down,
hair blowing in the wind—

just like one of those TikTok montages,
but with more heart and less choreography.

But Grandpa wasn't talking about singing.
He said I had a way of communicating.

"You might be a politician someday,"
he said. "You sure know how to talk."

At the time, I thought that meant I talked too much.
Now, I know he saw something I hadn't grown into yet.

As I got older, more people echoed it.
Teachers.
Coaches.
Even strangers.

They said I had a voice that made people listen.
That I was born to give a voice to the voiceless.

For a long time, I wasn't sure what that meant.
How do you give a voice to others
when you're still trying to find your own?

It's taken me decades, detours,
and more than one messy breakdown to realize:
you don't have to have all the answers to start speaking your
truth.

You just have to be willing to show up with it.

So this—this is me showing up.

This is me using the voice I was told was my gift.
Not to perform,
not to persuade,
but to finally tell my story.

You're going to read things
I've only ever shared with one or two people—if that.

Stories I've buried under
shame,
silence,
or "it wasn't that bad" for far too long.

This book isn't polished.
It's not perfectly healed.
But it's honest.
And that, I've learned, is enough.

I don't know about the politics business.
Honestly, that part still scares me.
Not because I don't care—
but because it's so often loud, cruel, and divisive.

It brings out the ugliest parts of people.
The parts that want to follow party lines
more than they want to be human.

I've seen politics weaponized in churches,
in schools,
in family group texts—
and I've learned that silence
sometimes feels safer than showing up.

But maybe that's the point.
Maybe the reason it scares me
is because somewhere deep down,
I know I can't stay silent.
Not forever.
Not when the stakes are people's
bodies, rights, lives, and stories.

I don't need to be an expert in everything.
But I do know what feels right.
And what doesn't.

And the thing is—
I've never fit neatly in one box.
I'm politically fluid.
I vote with my gut,
my values,
and the people I love in mind.
And that doesn't always follow party lines.

And as much as I've thought about stepping in—
really stepping in—
putting myself through the brutal process
of an election is one thing...
dragging my family along for the ride?
That doesn't feel like the kind of sacrifice I want to make.

Still, maybe that's the point.

Maybe the fear isn't the problem.
Maybe it's the invitation.
To speak up when it counts.
To lead in ways that feel aligned.

To remember that being a changemaker
doesn't always mean being on a ballot—
sometimes it just means
refusing to stay quiet.

Maybe the real courage
is using your voice even when it trembles.

So here I am.
Voice shaking.
Showing up.

My Gift Playlist:

"The Story" – Brandi Carlile
"Fearless" – Kat Perkins

Bonus Track:
"It's All Coming Back to Me Now" – Celine Dion

My Gift Reflection:

There's a moment in each of our lives
when someone sees something in us
before we see it ourselves.
A spark.
A gift.
A truth.

Sometimes it's a whisper we ignore.
Sometimes it's a roar we bury.
But it's always there, waiting for us to come back and claim it.

Your voice doesn't have to be loud to be powerful.
It doesn't have to be perfect to be true.
And it doesn't have to match anyone else's to be worth hearing.

What's one thing you've always been told you were "good at"
that maybe you didn't fully believe?

- Who told you?
- What did you make it mean at the time?
- What do you know about it now?

And if you could speak one truth today—just one—what would
it be?

Write it.
Say it.
Whisper it to yourself if you need to.

But let it live outside of you.

DISC ONE: Off the Record

DISC ONE: Off the Record

Before I found my voice,
I learned how to listen.

To the rules that shaped me,
the whispers that warned me,
the walls that held what I wasn't ready to name.

Silence was my first language.
Instinct was my second.

Off the record was where I kept
Everything that mattered most—
the stories I folded small enough
to slip between the cracks
so no one could take them from me.

DISC ONE Playlist

"Unwritten" – Natasha Bedingfield

Track 1 Girl Under the Stairs

How did I get here?

I ask myself that a lot.

Not in the metaphorical life path way—
but in the literal,
how did I get under the stairs at school
with him during track practice kind of way.

I think we were supposed to be running bleachers.
Or maybe lifting weights.

I was on the varsity track team.
Sixth grade.
Even have a few blue ribbons
tucked in the old ribbon box I inherited from my grandpa—
his ribbons beside mine,
proof that I could throw.

That I was strong.
Valuable.
Watched.

But somehow, I got pulled off course—
diverted—
right into that shadowy pocket
under the stairs outside the history room.

Right into him.

I don't remember anyone noticing we were gone.

Not the coach.
Not the teammates.
Not even the building—
which seemed to lean away, like it couldn't bear to be a witness.

Like it had seen this before... and still couldn't watch.

This wasn't the first time.

I wish it were.
Not with him.
Not for me.

I was six or seven the first time something like this happened,
and I spoke up.
I told someone.

And of course, he said I was lying.
Of course he did.

That moment—
when truth was met with disbelief—
wasn't just a moment.
It was a blueprint.
It laid down the track
for how I'd walk through future betrayals:
quietly,
inwardly,
without expecting protection.
Or justice.

Because once you're labeled a liar
for telling the truth,
you stop wasting your breath.

Eight more times.
That's how many more times it happened.
With different boys.

I won't call them men—they didn't earn that title.

And honestly—
there were probably even more than eight.
I just can't remember.

Every time I start counting,
tracing the timeline back,
I stop.

Because I don't want to remember.
Not all of it.
Not again.

Some of them I barely remember,
mostly because of alcohol.
Alcohol didn't just blur the moments.
It blurred me.

It made it easier for them to take what they wanted
and easier for others to look the other way.

It hid me—
not just from the outside world,
but from myself.
It gave them an alibi.
And it gave me shame.

Not because I did anything wrong—
but because I couldn't prove I didn't.

Eventually, the fear of what they'd do to me if I told someone
outweighed the hope that anyone would believe me.

So I stayed quiet.
Swallowed whole
by silence that wasn't mine.

One night, highly intoxicated,
I went home with a guy whose name I never knew.
A blur of a face I couldn't place even if I tried.

My dear friend Laurie insisted on going with me—
My quiet guardian.
Some part of her must've felt what I couldn't say out loud.

She always seemed to know
when I was in over my head.
When I was too hurt, too numb, too lost
to protect myself.

I don't remember much.
Just waking up,
wondering where I was.

The smell of stale beer.
The sting of regret in my throat.

I threw up in his tape collection.
(That detail I remember vividly—
a strange kind of justice
for whatever had or hadn't happened.)

I found Laurie sleeping
on the bachelor infested couch downstairs
and whispered that I wanted to go home.

She nodded, didn't ask questions.
Thank God.
She didn't ask.
And I didn't have to lie.

There are some friendships that save you
without needing to be named as salvation.
Laurie was that for me.

Another time was at a wedding dance
in a small town in South Dakota.

Everyone was on the floor doing the alligator.
I crouched down to join in,
then turned to my friend and said
I was leaving to go to a party with a guy
I'd met the last time I was in town.

I had been drinking before we left,
but I wasn't intoxicated.
Not even close.

The last thing I remember
is sitting in the backseat of a car,
wedged between two people.

The next thing I knew,
I was waking up on the floor of a strange house.
The lighting was strange—
maybe blue,
maybe just cold—
and there was a lamp on the ground.

No blankets.

No furniture.

Just a body
that didn't feel like mine anymore.

The next morning I woke up
with atrocious hickies all over my neck.
Big purple reminders—
bruises in the shape of someone else's actions.

Evidence of something
I didn't choose,
couldn't stop,
and couldn't even remember.

And I know what some people might be thinking:
You'd been drinking.
So maybe it was your fault.
That tired, cruel narrative.

I wasn't wearing anything "provocative."
I've never even owned anything "sexy."
Just jeans.
Maybe a dress shirt.

It would be the last time my guard—
and my voice—was down.

Some memories are clearer than others.

Eventually, I learned.
Too much.
Too soon.

The most sinister thing about manipulation
is how soft it can sound.

They say the right things in the right voice
at the wrong time,
and suddenly,
you're the one who feels guilty.

Like you offered this.
Like you invited harm.
Like your existence is what needs to be questioned.

The instances that occurred while I was a minor—
none of them were more than five years older than me,
so they didn't check the ACE score box.

(ACE stands for Adverse Childhood Experiences—
a tool used to assess trauma through
a checklist of specific events like abuse, neglect, or household
dysfunction.)

Funny how trauma tries to get quantified like that.
Like pain has to pass a standardized test to be valid.

Not that it mattered anyway.
I wasn't going to tell anyone.

But if you've ever found yourself under the stairs—
physically,
emotionally,
metaphorically—
you know.

You know what it means to go still and small.

You know what it feels like
to try and disappear
before someone else decides to make you disappear first.

And maybe,
like me,

you've blamed yourself.

You've tried to stitch timelines
and justifications together
into something that makes it all make sense.

But here's the truth:
The girl under the stairs
didn't put herself there.
She was placed there by a world
that didn't listen when she first said,
"Something happened."

She was quiet,
not because she was weak,
but because silence was the only thing
that had ever protected her.

Until now.

Somewhere,
deep in the silence of that staircase,
I learned that speaking up could be dangerous.

So I didn't.

I learned that being still might keep me safe.

So I was.

But safety built on silence
is a safety that cages you.

Sometimes,
I think I'm glad I never said anything.

Because even back then,
girls who spoke up—
or worse, girls who didn't survive—
were the ones picked apart.

She was too much.
Too fast.
She shouldn't have been out that late.
Shouldn't have worn that.
Shouldn't have trusted him.

There was a girl found in the park.
He said she wanted it.
She didn't live to say otherwise.

He was handsome,
came from a good family.
They worried about his future.
Her name became a warning.

But not for boys.

I was too young to understand it all,
but old enough to feel
the lesson underneath:
Speak, and they'll shame you.
Stay quiet, and at least they'll leave you alone.

And now,

I see it hasn't changed much.

A girl tells her truth
and suddenly she's an accuser—
as if naming the harm
makes her the one causing it.

I've watched women break open in courtrooms,
and somehow they're the ones on trial.

Their past.
Their clothing.
Their tone of voice.

I've seen young girls testify
against powerful men
and get treated like liars
for not being perfect victims.

And the one who named royalty?
She got dragged through headlines
like she was the one
with something to hide.

They twist survivors into destroyers.
Make our voices sound like weapons.

Our truth—
a threat.

Back then,
I thought silence was survival.

Now I know it was armor.
Heavy.
Suffocating.
But the only thing I had.

And then came 2024.

I hired Coach Tiff.
A spunky 5-foot former CIA agent,
American Gladiator runner-up,
and unapologetic truth-slayer.
With her sharp insights,
louder-than-life presence,
and gravity-defying spiked hair,
that made her easily look 7-foot-4.

That woman
could spot a limiting belief across state lines.
You'll hear about her again in this book—
she left her fingerprints all over the blueprint of my becoming.

Part of her coaching program
included a two-day intensive in San Diego.

It was there that I finally met the girl under the stairs again—
but this time,
through the eyes of a woman
ready to rewrite the story.

What I Learned:

REWIRE: SPEAKING MY TRUTH = MORE SAFETY,
MORE LOVE

BEFORE:
I learned early on that silence wasn't weakness—
it was protection.

What happened to me was absolutely f'ng terrible—
something no one should ever have to experience.
And at the time,
my mind and body did exactly what they needed to do
to protect me.
Go silent.
Go still.
Stay safe.

And for that,
I honor little me.
She survived.
She did everything right

NOW:
Now, I know that alignment—
living in my truth—
leads to deeper love,
stronger belonging,
and yes,
even more safety with the right people.

The new truth I'm choosing to live by.

RELEASING THE FEELS:
You can't rewrite a story
while holding your breath.
You have to exhale.
I didn't expect to go that deep at the intensive—

but I did.

And once I let myself open up,
the weight I'd been carrying for years
started to shift.

That's always the hardest part:
allowing it to rise instead of shoving it back down.
And this time,
I didn't run.
I faced it.

Now, I practice tune-ups—
shaking meditations,
daily stillness,
and tracking the moment
that a trigger creeps into my chest like a whisper.

When it shows up,
I no longer default to autopilot.

I pause.

I tell my inner little girl:
You are safe.
This is not that.

I TAKE ACTION WHEN THE FROG SHOWS UP:
These days,
when I feel the frog in my throat,
I know what it means.

Now, when my throat tightens

and my breath shortens,
I don't ignore it.
I don't push through.
I listen.

That sensation is the body's way of saying:
pause,
feel,
speak.

It's my body screaming:
Give little Nicole some love!

So I do.

I check in.
I see her.
I give her what she needs.
And then I return to the moment—
this one—
not the one from the stairs.

I assume good of myself,
and others,
and I speak.
Because my voice isn't just a tool.
It's my gift.
And I'm done hiding it.

Letter to the Girl Under the Stairs:

Dear You,

I see you.
Curled in a space too small for your voice,
too dim for your light.
Holding your breath because it feels safer
than asking to be heard.

You don't know it yet,
but what you're doing isn't weakness—
it's survival.
It's brilliance.
It's the sacred instinct of a soul refusing to disappear,
even when the world tries to shrink you down.

You think you're hiding.
But you're actually anchoring.
Creating the smallest space in the world
where you still belong to yourself.

I wish I could crawl under there with you—
not to pull you out,
but to let you know you're not alone.

That one day,
the very voice you're silencing
will be the one that sets others free.

You will not always feel this lost.
This ashamed.
This unsure whether the things that happened to you
somehow make you the one at fault.
They don't.

You didn't deserve any of it.

And the fact that you're still here,
still breathing,
still soft enough to hope?
That's your superpower.

When you are ready—
you will rise.
Not because someone rescues you,
but because you remember
you were never the one who needed saving.

With love,
Me
(The one who grew up and came back for you)

What I Wish Someone Would've Told Me Then

- You are not to blame for what someone else chose to do. Full stop.
- Just because no one believed you once doesn't mean your truth isn't still worth speaking.
- Manipulation isn't always loud. Sometimes it sounds like flattery. Sometimes it wears a familiar face.
- You don't owe silence to anyone who hurt you.
- Healing won't be linear. You'll feel strong one day and gutted the next. Both are part of the process.
- Forgiveness doesn't mean forgetting. And it never means pretending it didn't matter.
- You're allowed to be angry. You're allowed to name what happened. You're allowed to stop protecting the people who didn't protect you.

- One day, your story will be a lifeline for someone else.
- And maybe the most important one: You were never broken. Just buried. And girl–you are already digging yourself out.

Girl Under the Stairs Playlist

"Breathe Me" – Sia
"I Know a Place" – MUNA
"Praying" – Kesha.
"In Dreams" – Jai-Jagdeesh This was the song Coach Tiff shared with me during the intensive. It broke me wide open. Soft. Soulful. Sacred. Like a lullaby for the part of me that finally felt safe enough to be seen.

Girl Under the Stairs Reflection:

Were there places you used to hide—
physically or emotionally?

When was the first time you remember feeling invisible, dismissed, or disbelieved?

What did you learn about your voice growing up? Was it welcome, or too loud, too much, too inconvenient?

Is there a part of your story you've never spoken out loud? What would it feel like to name it?

What does safety mean to you now? How has that changed from what it meant as a child?

What do you need today to feel safe enough to speak your truth—
even if it shakes?

When something uncomfortable rises in your body (like a tight throat, closed chest, or clenching), what is it trying to tell you?

Track 2 Little Girl in the Pew

I don't remember the sermon word-for-word.

But I remember the feeling.
That awful ache in my chest,
like a wrecking ball of shame
hit the one place I thought was still safe.

Like every word the pastor said
was a stone being thrown
at a version of me I hadn't even met yet.

There I was—
knees pressed together,
hands folded just right,
trying to hold it all in
while the man with the microphone talked about sin.

About perversion.
About how "people like that"

needed to repent or burn.

I didn't have the language yet.
I just knew I felt...different.

And in that pew,
the same one we sat in every Sunday,
surrounded by hymns, handshakes
and people who smelled like coffee and Aqua Net—
I learned that "different" meant "unacceptable",
and that love
had fine print I'd never be able to meet.

That love came with conditions.
That being "good"
meant being quiet.

No one said my name.
No one had to.

The words weren't aimed at me directly,
but they found their mark–
A direct hit to my heart.

I spent years
trying to become the kind of girl churches would bless.

I even joined JC & Company in college—
yes, that's the actual name—
and we traveled around performing in churches on Sundays.
Singing about love.
About grace.
About the God I never stopped believing in,

even when His followers
made me feel like an abomination.

Here's the wild part:
I still love God.
I love Jesus.
I even love Christians—
real ones.
The kind who embody Christ.
The kind who show up with humility and open arms.
The kind who understand that love doesn't come
with a terms-and-conditions contract.

But religious people?
The ones who weaponize scripture
to justify their own discomfort or control?
Some of them are just mean.

They say things that echo in the mind
long after the service ends.
They shame in the name of sanctity.
They use pulpits like podiums for judgment.
And it wrecks people.

And then there are the social media bios.
They say...
"Love Jesus."
"God first."
"Saved by grace."

But then they post things that reek of cruelty.
They judge.
Mock.

Shame.
They say things
I can't imagine Jesus ever co-signing.

And I can't help but wonder—
Are they trying to convince me?
Themselves?
Or God Himself?

Because real love doesn't need a caption to prove it.
And real faith isn't performative.

Sometimes, I think people cling to those bios
like they're bargaining chips.

As if they post enough verses
and say the right things in public,
Jesus will overlook what they're hiding in private.

But that's not faith.
That's fear in a filter.

Some of the deepest cuts
don't come from pulpits.
They come from the people
you once called "friend".

The ones you stayed up late with,
sharing dreams and doubts.

The ones who hugged you
through heartbreak
and knew your favorite I-90 order by mid-semester.

You sang together,
studied together,
maybe even prayed together.

Years later,
they post memes about
"traditional marriage"
like it's a punchline.

Or share political rants
about how "marriage is only between a man and a woman"
like they're reciting a moral victory speech.

And it hurts.
Not because I need their approval—
but because part of me still remembers loving them.
Trusting them.

It's not just a difference of opinion
when your identity is on the line.
It's personal.
It's piercing.

I don't need them to agree with every part of who I am.
But I do need them to remember
that who I am is still human.
Still worthy.
Still the same girl
who held space for their dreams and wiped their tears.

Sometimes I want to scream:
Do you know who you're talking about when you hit "share"?
Do you remember I'm still here—

reading that post,
absorbing that judgment?

I know not everyone evolves at the same pace.
But I also know silence in the face of harm is complicity.
And some of those posts?
They're not just disappointing.
They're devastating.

I carried that "I am bad" belief for decades.
Not because I was,
but because I learned–
early, often, and with a spiritual smile—
that my truth made people uncomfortable.
And uncomfortable people
can be cruel.

But even in the heaviness,
there were moments—
tiny flickers—
that felt like grace.
Not the kind they preached about
with fire and fear,
but the kind that wrapped around me
like a warm quilt in a cold pew.

There was one song
that didn't feel like a threat—
didn't make me small,
didn't make me bad.
Because He Lives.

I don't remember the first time I heard it,

but I remember how it felt.
Like a soft place to land
when everything else was sharp.

They sang it in that little church
with cracked hymnals and cracked theology,
but the words floated higher
than the judgment in the room.

Because He lives,
I can face tomorrow.
I used to hum it
when tomorrow felt like too much.
When the silence of shame
was louder than any choir,
I clung to that chorus
like a life raft.
It didn't matter that the verses
were wrapped in a story
I didn't know if I believed anymore.

The melody held me.
The hope saved me.
The message—
that life was still worth living
because of something bigger—
somehow,
that was enough.

It would be years
before I'd untangle that kind of faith
from the fear it was packaged in.

But that song?
It didn't come from fear.
It came from survival.

From something inside me
still worth saving.

And for a while,
I stopped singing.
Stopped trusting.
Stopped showing up.
But deep down,
I never stopped listening.

I didn't have the words for any of this as a kid.
I just knew my body kept the score.
My chest got tight.
My breath got small.
My truth felt dangerous.

At my coaching intensive with Tiff,
we traced those feelings
all the way back to that pew.
She said,
"This had to feel absolutely terrible...
beyond terrible—
and probably terrifying."
She wasn't wrong.

I didn't just fear being judged—
I feared being rejected
by the people who claimed to speak for God.
I didn't just fear their judgment.

I feared divine rejection—
that God Himself
might not want someone like me.

And when you're young,
the idea that God might not want you?
It doesn't just hurt—
it lingers in the background of everything.

Now, when I feel that familiar pressure in my chest—
that panicky,
rushing feeling—
I know what it is.

It's a red alert from little me.
She's back in that pew,
terrified that truth equals danger.

So I pause.

I see her.

I whisper,
"I got you."

I tell her,
"It's safe now.
Our truth is not bad.
Our truth is beautiful.
And it has every right
to take up space."

I haven't stepped foot in that church for years.

But its messages?
They stepped into me—
and stayed.

They plowed the building down
a few years back—
asbestos, they said.
I wondered if shame
was hiding in the walls too.
If they bulldozed the pew
where I sat small and silent,
swallowing guilt like communion.

Funny how a building can burn
without fire—
just the weight of what it held.

And then I speak.
Not for vengeance.

Not for applause.
But because staying silent
in the face of shame
is no longer an option.

Little Girl in the Pew Playlist

"Take Me to Church" – Hozier
"You Say" – Lauren Daigle
"Secrets" – Mary Lambert
"Because He Lives" – Celtic Worship

Little Girl in the Pew Reflection:

Have you ever received a message—
spoken or unspoken—
that made you feel like who you are was "wrong" or "unacceptable"?
What was the setting?

What spiritual or moral beliefs shaped how you saw yourself growing up? Are they still true for you now?

Is there a younger version of you who learned to stay quiet in order to feel loved or safe? What would you say to them today?

How do you define unconditional love now?

What does it feel like in your body when a part of you feels "unacceptable"? Can you identify the sensation?

Track 3 Wild to the Roots

This chapter plays like an old-school mixtape—
full of short tracks that bleed into each other,
telling a story not through one melody, but many.

Each mini track stands on its own,
but together, they hum a deeper truth.
You'll find songs, reflections, and pieces of me
that never fit in a straight line—
but always found the beat.

TRACK 3.1 BARN BOARDS AND BOOM BOXES

I didn't throw dainty birthday parties with tiaras and tea sets.

There weren't neat rows of cupcakes with perfectly piped
frosting,
or make-up tutorials whispered between pink walls.

I wasn't that kind of kid.

We threw sleeping bags over our heads and ran blind through
the house,
crashing into furniture,
squealing like wild things,
laughing so hard it hurt.

We made up music videos before MTV even existed—
screaming lyrics into hairbrushes,
leaping off couches like we were headlining a world tour.

But it wasn't just for laughs.

I was always choreographing the next talent show in my head—
mapping out moves and costumes for "Monster Mash",
rewriting the words to "Manic Monday" into "Manic School
Day" (wish it was cartoon day),
practicing every step like it mattered.

Later, even babysitting turned into full-blown productions—
teaching the kids how to do the Locomotion,
running mini rehearsals in living rooms like some pint-sized
show director.

When the music ran out, the games started:
Kick the Can under the streetlights,
Hope to See the Ghost Tonight whispered with wide eyes,
and long, dusty sessions of Little House on the Prairie.

We fought over who got to be Ma and Pa,
turning old abandoned houses into our homesteads,
gathering twigs for fires we never lit,

patching invisible holes in the roofs with scraps and stubbornness.

We weren't just playing survival.
We were rehearsing it.

I wasn't made for dress-up parties.
I was made for bruised shins,
bare feet slapping pavement,
pretend tornado drills in the middle of the yard,
and daring the boys to let me ride the steers with them—
not just watch from the fence.

We weren't pretending to be wild.
We already were.

Even then, I knew—
freedom wasn't handed down.
It was carved out of laughter, scraped knees,
and a thousand made-up songs
that no one else may ever hear.

Barn Boards and Boom Boxes Playlist:

"Manic Monday" – Bangles
"Locomotion" – Kylie Minogue

Barn Boards and Boom Boxes Reflection:

Think back to your own childhood soundtracks.
What songs, games, or makeshift adventures shaped you—
before the world told you how you were supposed to be?

What wildness did you carry before you learned the word "responsibility"?

What parts of that scrappy, joyful, imagination still lives inside you now—
waiting to be heard again?

TRACK 3.2 THE TV WAS MY STAGE

I was five the day my grandpa and I went rummage sale hunting.
He was a treasure finder—
the kind of man who could see gold where others saw junk.

But that day, it was my eyes
that caught the glint: a little black-and-white TV, dusty and scuffed, sitting on a folding table next to mismatched cups and a cracked lamp.
I looked up at him, wide-eyed, and asked,
"Can I have it?"
He nodded, and just like that, it was mine.

That TV wasn't just a box of static and rabbit ears.
It was my portal—
to a world where people wore rubber heads and pretended to be aliens.

Where a man named Gumby could stretch and twist and bounce back,
where the Coneheads claimed to be "from France" but we all knew they weren't,

where Mr. Robinson's Neighborhood taught me about life in a
way that felt funnier—
and maybe even truer—
than the real Mr. Rogers.

I was five.
And I was hooked.

I didn't know it at the time,
but I wasn't just watching sketches.
I was studying characters—
the misfits, the oddballs, the sidekicks with a punchline.

I loved Stuart Smalley, who told me, "I'm good enough, I'm
smart enough, and doggone it, people like me."
I wanted to pump it up with Hans and Franz,
sit in the pews with Church Lady,
and maybe—
just maybe—
find my own way to make people laugh so hard it hurt.

I didn't understand the jokes sometimes—
but I understood the energy.
The way it felt when the music started,
when the cast ran on stage,
when the crowd roared,
when the lights dimmed and the world turned into anything-
can-happen.

I'd try so hard to stay awake on Saturday nights.
I'd prop my eyes open, willing myself to make it through the show,
to hear the Gunsmoke theme song

that followed SNL—
that was the finish line.

But without fail, I'd fall asleep mid-show and someone would
turn off the TV.
I'd wake up moments later and turn it right back on.
Because I had to see how the show ended.
I had to feel like I was part of that world.
Even at five years old, I knew—
this wasn't just a show I watched.
This was a calling.

It's why I'd invent my own characters—
like the "Sure, ya, you betchya girl"—
a sassy, Midwestern sweetheart with a wink, a casserole and a
story for everything.
It's why I'd practice sketches in the mirror.

It's why I turned a psych paper into a compilation of my
favorite Jack Handey quotes
when the teacher said we could write about anything.

It's why, one year, my friends and I took a ski trip with an SNL
theme.
We pulled over randomly on the side of the road to reenact
skits—
cheerleaders, Mary Katherine Gallagher, Delicious Dish—you
name it.
Yes, it's all on video.
And yes, we committed.

It wasn't just about the TV.
It was about possibility.

It was about feeling seen by an audience
that didn't know I existed,
and somehow, still believing I could belong in that world.

Even when I was little, I knew—
this wasn't just a show I watched.
It was a part of who I was becoming.

It's why, at 50, I dressed up like Sally O'Malley—
kicking and stretching—
not just for a laugh,
but because I could.

Because that little girl with the secondhand TV
never really left.
She just grew into someone who knew
the power of stepping into a character,
of taking up space,
of making the world laugh.

The TV Was My Stage Playlist

"Saturday Night Live" – John Batiste

The TV Was My Stage Reflection

What was the show or obsession that first made you feel seen—
even when you didn't know exactly why?

Was it a song, a character, a story, a movie?

What did it teach you about yourself, about possibility, about
where you belonged?

And if you close your eyes for a moment...
can you still hear the music playing?

TRACK 3.3 CASES WE NEVER SOLVED

We weren't the kind of kids who spent our summers braiding
each other's hair
or planning our wedding colors.

Pam and I had bigger missions.

We'd stock up on fake candy cigarettes,
ride our bikes down to the post office,
and pull up the collars of our jackets
like detectives in the movies.

Inside, pinned to the wall by the community bulletin board,
were layers of missing-kids posters.

Faces that looked just like ours.
Some smiling.
Some serious.
Some already starting to fade.

We'd stand there for what felt like hours,
studying the names,
memorizing the descriptions,
making a plan.
Then we'd jump on our bikes and set out—

circling the town
like it was our personal case file.

Looking in alleys,
behind bushes,
under porches.

Not pretending.

Searching.

We didn't just play detective.
We believed we could actually find them.
We thought maybe, if we pedaled fast enough,
or looked hard enough,
or cared enough,
we could bring somebody home.

And somehow,
that made the world feel less broken—
for a little while.

Cases We Never Solved Playlist

"Somewhere Only We Know" – Keane

Cases We Never Solved Reflection

When we were kids, what we called "games" were often
rehearsals for something deeper.

Maybe we weren't just playing.

Maybe we were practicing how to run, how to lead, how to hope, how to survive.

What were the games you played as a child that, looking back now,
taught you something real about the world you were about to face?

TRACK 3.4 GHOSTS AND GUITARS

I learned early that not all tragedies make a sound.
Some live in quiet stories nobody tells.

I lost my Uncle Donnie the day before my first birthday.
A tragic car accident caused by an intoxicated driver.

I didn't know him—
barely knew stories of him—
until much later.
He lived, at first, in the silent spaces—
the ones where families keep the sharp memories they don't know how to touch.

His name floated like a ghost at family gatherings,
more presence than shared stories.

All I knew of him
came from a few pictures
and a letter of commendation from the U.S. military—
stories about bravery,
about jumping out of planes,
about living loud.

Many years later,
my mom would start to share.
About the Mustang he drove.
About the band he played in.
About the way he lived like fear was something other
people had.

You could hear it in her voice—
the way she looked up to him.
The way she adored him.
Like he wasn't just her brother.
He was a star stitched right into her sky.

I inherited his guitar.
A six-stringed ghost.
A story I never got to live,
but somehow,
still got to carry.

Sometimes, the people who shape us most
are the ones we never even get to meet.

Their absence carves space inside you—
a place where legacy hums,
even when you don't know the song.

Ghosts and Guitars Playlist

"Wish You Were Here" – Pink Floyd

Ghosts and Guitars Reflection

Who are the people you never got to meet—
but still feel tied to?

What family stories were passed down in whispers or scraps,
not full sentences?

Is there an object, a song, or a story that carries a memory bigger
than you?

If you could sit down with them—
what's one thing you would want to know?

What part of you do you think they would recognize immediately?

TRACK 3.5 WATCHING FOR HER

I couldn't believe it.

I had a sister.

A real sister.

It felt like something out of a dream—
too good,
too big,
too brand new to be real.

I remember the day she was born,
my six–year-old chest barely able to hold the excitement,

my voice a skipping record:
"I can't believe I have a sister.
I can't believe I have a sister."

Over and over,
like maybe if I said it enough,
it would stay real.

The day Mom and Dad brought her home,
I took over Grandma's spot on her stool
by the big picture window.
The perch where she usually sat,
watching the world arrive and unfold.
But that day, it was mine.
I must have sat there for hours—
or at least, it felt like hours—
waiting,
watching,
stretching my heart out toward the snowy Highway 3
where everything was about to change.

And when they pulled up,
it was like watching a miracle
unfold in the driveway.

My sister.
My sister.

The one person who has
always been there for me.

Before best friends.

Before first heartbreaks.

Before diplomas
and detours
and every road I would ever wander—
there was her.

Love wasn't new to me.
I had a little brother—
a love that was already stitched into my days.

But this time,
I was old enough to witness it.
To wait for it.
To feel my heart stretch on purpose.

My sister didn't replace anything.
She just opened something new.

She didn't make me love more—
she just made me realize
how much my heart could stretch
when it wanted to.

Watching for Her Playlist

"Count on Me" - Bruno Mars

Watching for Her Reflection

Can you remember a moment when love arrived in your life so big and new, it didn't feel quite real at first?

Who has been your "always" person—
the one whose presence stitched through every season of your
life?

TRACK 3.6 INDEPENDENT AF

I could walk, talk,
and pee in a pot by nine months old.

Diaper? Optional.

I'd rip it off and neatly set it in the corner of my crib
like a retirement notice.

No one taught me how to ride a bike.
I propped it next to the tailgate,
wriggled my way up,
and launched into the neighbor's yard—
a tiny Evel Knievel with skinned knees
and no brakes.

At five, I opened my first business:
a car wash for the bankers
and their patrons.
Armed with a bucket, a rag,
and the confidence of a CEO.
Pretty sure I left streaks on every car.
I debated not even mentioning this
in this book in case I owe some people for a paint job. (Sorry.)

I don't remember how much money I made.

That wasn't the point.

Having a great idea was the point.
Starting something.
Doing it myself.
Making it real.
That part lit me up.

Still does.

Maybe I had to be independent.

Maybe I was helping my parents out without even knowing it.

They had me young—
Mom was 16, Dad was 18.
I didn't know that until I was 16 myself,
sitting with the math in my lap
like it had just done a magic trick.

I'm the first woman in at least four generations
not to have a baby before age twenty.
My running joke is that my mom
was probably crocheting a baptismal gown
as my high school graduation gift.

No one had hidden it.
But no one had said it out loud either.
And suddenly,
so many things made sense—
and none of them changed.

Because even before I knew their ages,

I knew something wasn't typical.

The way I learned to handle things.
The way I didn't ask twice.
The way I could sense when they needed me
to not need anything.

I used to think independence was my superpower.

But maybe it was also my offering.

My quiet way of helping
before I knew what help even meant.

Independent AF Playlist

"Fast Car" – Tracy Chapman

Independent AF Reflection

What part of your independence was chosen?

And what part was handed to you before you could say no?

TRACK 3.7 BREAKING THE BANK

They told me stories—
how my piggy bank
paid for groceries,
kept the trailer lit.

Dad worked sunup
to sundown,
and maybe longer—
or that's how it felt.

If we wanted to see him,
we packed supper
and found him in the field.
Wheat between my teeth,
chewed to gum.
A few rounds in the combine—
Dad and me, or Grandpa.
Just us, some dust,
diesel and sky.

My dad is a quiet guy.
His actions did the talking—
if they said anything at all.

I can only remember
one time he talked non-stop:
driving home from a town dance
with a car full of my girlfriends.

He kept asking what kind of dancing that was.
Back in my day, he said,
we danced to Jeremiah Was a Bulldog (this is not a typo).
We howled.
He grinned.
That drive still makes me smile.

And then there was the day
we almost launched a tractor

into space.

My brother,
my cousin,
and I
were playing in the farmyard—
as wild and unsupervised
as any good '80s childhood.

Yelling out every few minutes,
"Hey, Dad—look at this!"
He was brushing my horse,
barely looking up—
just waved,
probably for the hundredth time.

Next thing you know,
someone was shifting gears on the tractor.

It might've been my cousin.
Could've been my brother.
Surely couldn't have been me.

But the loader caught the angle just right,
and we started climbing.
Steel beneath us,
Quonset curving like it was daring us.

I don't remember how we stopped.
Just that no one died,
and somehow,
Dad still didn't yell.
He was quiet like that—

steady,
grit in his gaze,
soft where it counted.

He didn't have to say much.
You just felt it.

I remember the first time
He told me he loved me.

I was heading back to South Dakota
for college—
trying to beat a winter storm.
I wasn't gone eight hours
when Grandma—his mom—
passed away.
Cancer.

I couldn't make it back for the funeral.
The storm wouldn't let up.
One of Dad's friends even offered
to drive all 308 miles
with his tractor to get me.

I didn't make it back.
But I heard the words.
Finally.
Through grief,
through storm,
through that quiet kind of love
that takes its time
but never runs out.

Our parents were also our bus drivers.
Dad took the first half
until he hit our stop—
right on cue
with the Bozo Show
Grand Prize Game.
Then Mom took the wheel.

Mom was the backbone.
The one who held the whole thing together
with grit, grace, and just enough side-eye
to keep the world in check.

She never drank when we were growing up.
People would offer her a beer,
and she'd smile and say,
"No thanks. Last time I had a beer, I had Nicole."

It became a kind of family punchline.
A little lore.
Proof that I'd been fermenting in boldness since the womb.

I never saw her touch a drink—
not until after my brother was deployed to Iraq.

Even then, I didn't see it.
But I heard about it.
Heard how the world spun sideways after a few beers,
how quiet pain can sometimes get loud
when no one's watching.

But even then—
she got up the next morning,

made breakfast,
folded the towels,
and carried on like women do
when the world is burning
and there's still housework to be done.

Mom had quit school to raise me.
Married young.

But she wasn't done.
Back then, you had to ask the state for permission
to get your GED.
She did—
and they denied her.
Told her,
"You have a husband to take care of you."

She didn't fight back right away.
Not out loud, at least.

But years later,
once all her kids were in school,
she walked in,
took every test in a single day,
and passed them all.
Even a near-perfect score in Math.

No pomp and circumstance.
No speeches.
No applause.
Just a quiet middle finger
to the system that underestimated her.

I think she always wondered
what she could've done
if she hadn't had me so young.

But she did everything
our tiny town had to offer—
and she did it well.
Grocery clerk.
Postmaster.
City auditor.
Election poll worker.
EMT.
Grandma D's kitchen queen.
Sewing machine magician.
Name a job—
she showed up
and nailed it.

She never missed a moment—
Okay, maybe six or seven.
But who's counting?

Once, I came home
and she wasn't there.
I couldn't read,
so she left me
a tape-recorded message
that told me I was safe.

Once, I got out of the dentist chair
and she was gone.
I was sad and scared at first,
but less than five minutes later

you would find me working the front desk
like I owned the place.

Once, prom night.
Kari rode her bike
through barbed wire
trying to learn
before she was ready.
Our "mentoring" might have had
something to do with that.
Mom tended to her wounds
over my hair and makeup.

Some of the biggest moments, though—
the ones that cracked something in me—
were quieter.

When I came out
not once, but twice,
and needed her to stand beside me
when the world wouldn't.

And the time,
when I was little,
and she and the others
didn't take my side
about what happened
with that boy.

I don't think it was
because she didn't love me.

She just didn't know how yet.

We didn't say
I love you
out loud.

But I always knew.
Still do.

My kids hear it
a hundred times a day.
I make sure of it—
every goodbye,
every car door click.

In high school,
rumors were as thick as gravel.
One was that I was moving to Mandan
to live with my real mom.
Another that I was on steroids.

In our tiny towns,
even the weekly paper
reported who poured coffee
at whose kitchen table.

Nothing stayed a secret.
But some things—
some things stayed silent.

Breaking the Bank Playlist

"The House That Built Me" – Miranda Lambert

Breaking the Bank Reflection:

Think back to the people who raised you.
Where did they show up without fail?

Where did they fall short—
not from lack of love, but maybe from lack of tools, timing, or
understanding?

How did those moments—both presence and absence—
shape the way you now show up for others?

And what would you say to that younger version of you,
waiting in the field, or at the dentist, or in the silence that
followed something that shouldn't have happened?

TRACK 3.8 GLOVES OFF

My brother and I—
we've always had
a boxing-gloves kind of bond.

Literally.
Our parents even bought us a pair.
We wore holes in them.

Close, sometimes.
Clashing, often.
Equal parts swing and silence.

He's told me—
more than once—

to keep my "social working ass"
out of his life.
(His words, not mine.)

So I try.
Most of the time.

Still—
I named my youngest son after him.
Nathan Mitchell.
Born just months
after he returned
from Iraq.

Some things
we don't say out loud.

But they're felt
just the same.

Like that night—
the one before my college graduation.
Also my birthday.
We were out—
music, friends, family,
a bar full of everything good.

Toward the end,
tears surprised me.
He saw.
And he asked—
"Is it a guy? I'll kick his ass."
"No. I don't cry over guys."

"Is it one of your friends?
Should I talk to them?"
"No, I love all of my friends."
"Then what's wrong?"
And I said—
"This is the happiest
and the saddest day of my life."

He didn't say a word.
Just nodded.
Like he knew.
Like maybe he felt it too.

Some things
we don't say out loud.
But they land
like a hand on your back
when the gloves come off.

Gloves Off Playlist

"Brother" – NEEDTOBREATHE

Gloves Off Reflection

What kind of gloves did your relationships come with?

Were they soft and open-palmed?
Closed fists and guarded silence?
Something in between?

Think about a sibling, cousin, or childhood friend who shaped you through conflict and connection.

TRACK 3.9 GARAGE SALE GAYS

I was the flower girl—
Peach dress with white lace trim,
basket full of flowers in sweaty palms.

He was the ring bearer.
Brother of my soon-to-be uncle.
Tiny tux, clip-on brown bow tie,
a shared dislike for following directions.

We ran off during rehearsal.
Two kids with better things to do
than walk in a straight line
toward a future we already knew
would bend.

They found us
at a garage sale down the street—
probably digging through
a box of mismatched action figures
and secondhand sequins.

I was four, he was seven or eight.
Clueless and clear—
we didn't know who we were,
but something in us already did.
Maybe, deep down,
We already knew we were both queer.
No labels, just light—

our true colors quietly shining through.

Now—
decades later—
we've both walked down aisles again.
Married the loves of our lives.
Living out loud—no clip-on ties, no disguises.
Just truth, finally dressed in our own skin.

From garage sales
to wedding vows,
we found our way
without ever fitting in a straight line.

Garage Sale Gays Playlist

"True Colors" – Cyndi Lauper

Garage Sale Gays Reflection:

What were the early hints
that you were different—
not broken,
not wrong,
just you?

Think back to the childhood moments
when your spirit showed up
before you even knew its name.

Where did you feel most free to be curious?
To wander?

To run off course
and find a garage sale instead of the aisle?

TRACK 3.10 SILENT UNDERSTANDING

Before I ever understood girls like me,
or had the words to name the ache,
I had a horse—
and she had me.

She looked at me
like she knew things.
Like maybe
she'd once been a young girl too—
misunderstood,
sensitive,
a little wild at the edges.

She held my stories
like reins—
loose enough to let me run,
tight enough to keep me safe.
She let me cry into her mane
more than once.

And when the world felt too loud,
she'd rest her heavy head
on my shoulder—
a gesture so soft
it felt like a hug
God forgot to teach people.

Fourth grade:
horse camp,
me and Holy Smoke—
my trusted steed
with the eyes of an old soul.

At camp, we skipped a few chores—
okay, we strategically avoided
chin hair trims.
She hated them.
I took the KP duty hit
without a second thought.
It was the least I could do
for the only soul
who saw me without flinching.

We danced in circles
around barrels,
walked the line of Western Pleasure—
never winning,
but always moving
at a rhythm that felt like ours.

Somewhere in there,
I roped a boy
to be my dance partner.

But let's be real—
the one who got my rhythm,
who matched my energy,
who stood by me without asking me to shrink.
The real partner,
the one who got my pace,

who knew my weight
and held it like grace—
was always waiting
at the fence for me.

Silent Understanding Playlist

"Wildflowers" – Dolly Parton, Emmylou Harris, Linda
Ronstadt
"Chasing Cars" – Snow Patrol

Silent Understanding Reflection

Who (or what) was your Holy Smoke?

Think back to a time when you felt truly seen—
not because someone said the right thing, but because they
didn't need to.

Was it a person, an animal, a place,
a moment so quiet it whispered to your soul: "You don't have to
change a thing."

Write them a letter.
You don't have to send it.

But let them know what their silent understanding meant to
the version of you that needed it most.

TRACK 3.11 SAINTS, SHILLELAGHS & BUTTERFINGER PIE

Some legacies are loud—
full of speeches, medals, or memoirs.

Mine came wrapped in bib overalls, puff paint, old-school
coffee mugs, and Butterfinger pie.

My grandparents weren't perfect.
They didn't always say the right thing—
some of them barely said anything at all.

But they showed up.
With grit, humor, and a kind of homemade magic
that stitched itself into my bones.

They taught me that strength could be silent,
love could be lumpy,
and pride didn't always look like gold stars—
sometimes it looked like wine that tasted terrible but was made
with pride.

This track is for the ones who raised me with their hands,
their stories,
and their strange but sacred ways.

TRACK 3.11.A WINDBREAKERS AND BOGGLE NIGHTS

Grandma Morrison didn't do reckless.
She was thoughtful, steady—

always a little cautious,
the kind of woman who read the fine print
and folded her towels just so.

So when she helped me make T-Bird jackets
for my friend Troy and me—
black windbreakers with orange puff paint—
I don't think she knew
We were forming our own little gang.

Inspired by Grease,
fueled by imagination,
and just enough rebellion to feel dangerous
in our elementary school bodies.

We put them on and hopped on our bikes,
riding around town like we had somewhere to be—
and no bedtime.

She thought she was helping with a craft.
We thought we were invincible.

When we weren't playing outlaw,
I was at her kitchen table,
sipping coffee
like I had bills to pay
and world news to debate.
We'd sit for hours—
me barely big enough to wrap my hands around the mug—
playing Boggle
like it was the most important championship of our lives.

She chewed her peas

one hundred times per pea.
Always the last one at the table.
Always making things last.
Even the quietest moments
became something sacred
just because she stayed with them.

She let me feel smart
and safe
and seen
without ever having to say it out loud.

That was her magic.
She didn't need to talk about love.
She just brewed it.

TRACK 3.11.B THOSE AREN'T CANDY

I smoked my Grandma Belile's Pall Malls once.
It didn't taste nearly as good as the candy cigarettes
Pam and I used when we were being detectives—
solving mysteries with powdered sugar on our lips
and absolutely zero adult supervision.

Flecks of tobacco clung to my tongue
like bitter confessions,
and the inhale burned more than just my throat—
it scorched something I didn't have words for yet.

I thought it would toughen me up.
Maybe it did.
Maybe it made me fireproof.

Or maybe I just learned how to keep breathing through the
burn.

She couldn't cook worth shit—
dry turkey; even her instant potatoes were lumpy,
green beans boiled into submission.

She made her own wine, too.
Poured it proudly from repurposed bottles
with homemade labels written in permanent marker.

It was terrible.
Tasted like fruit gone bad and good intentions.

We all drank it anyway.

Because she did it with pride—
like every glass was a love note,
even if it burned a little going in
and out.

But every Christmas,
without fail,
she made a Butterfinger pie
that could bring grown men to their knees.

It was legendary.
No recipe, just magic and muscle memory.
Somehow, she got that one thing exactly right.
And maybe that was enough.

TRACK 3.11.C MEET ME AT THE OLD HOUSE

When Grandpa Morrison left town,
he'd call me.

Just a simple, "Meet me at the old house."
And that was all I needed.
I'd run—
wind in my face,
heart thumping like it knew the way.

Two miles to the place where old stories
lived in the walls.
We'd load minnows and head out to the ice,
me, Dad, and Grandpa.

We sat for hours in that frozen silence—
fishing, hoping, waiting.
You didn't complain.
If you did, you didn't get invited back.

So I learned to read the lake.
Skated when I was bored,
talked to strangers in nearby shacks,
pretended I was on a mission.
I always made it an adventure.
Because it mattered too much not to.

He had a line he'd say when we were being naughty—
"I'm gonna go get a stick."
Always the stick.

Invisible, of course.
Sometimes he'd call it a shillelagh
like it came from some ancient Irish village
just to find our backsides.

We never actually saw it.
But we believed in it,
like you believe in Santa or God or karma.

One time, I decided I'd earned it—
deserved a good invisible whipping.
So I got bold.
Put a mousetrap in his boot—
thinking I'd teach him a lesson first.

Then, to test it out,
I put my own foot in the boot.
Snap.
Instant regret.
Lesson learned.
No one messes with Grandpa's shillelagh—
not even me.

TRACK 3.11.D SAINTS IN DISGUISE

Both of my Grandpas
played Santa
in their communities
for over fifty years.

Red suits, white beards, twinkling eyes—
not just for show,

but stitched into the fabric of who they were.

They didn't just pass out candy canes—
they handed out wonder.

They weren't just characters in a costume—
they were guardians
of something sacred and unseen.

The kind of men who showed up
when it mattered,
without needing a spotlight
to do the shining.

When my boys were little,
they only knew one of them—
Grandpa Morrison had passed before they were born.

But they saw photos.
Heard the stories.
And one Christmas,
after a quiet car ride home
after realizing Great-Grandpa Belile
was Santa.
I took them to see Rise of the Guardians.
That's when the magic clicked.
Not just the Santa suit—
but what it meant.

That they came from men
who made magic believable
not with sleigh bells,
but with presence.

That they came from guardians—
not just of holidays,
but of joy,
and generosity,
and the sacred art
of showing up.

TRACK 3.11.E FAST SHOES AND FLO JO

New shoes were currency.
Not just because they were clean,
but because they made me believe
I could outrun anything.

One time, Grandpa Belile asked,
"Let's see how fast those things go."
So I took off—
right through the mall—
arms pumping, heart flying,
like I was chasing the Olympics.
Like Flo Jo in a Kmart track suit.

And when I turned back,
he was smiling like I had just won something real.
Maybe I had.

TRACK 3.11.F SUMMER GROWN-UP

With Grandpa Belile, summer didn't smell like sunscreen—
it smelled like hay, spit tobacco, sweat,
and something alive in the dirt.

I drank black coffee in chipped mugs,
and helped toss bales like I had something to prove.

Watched horses be born,
chickens be butchered.
I didn't flinch.
I wanted him to see I could handle it.
By ten, I was the fastest chicken-gutter in the county.

And when he let me paint "o1" on that wheelless car out back,
I didn't just paint numbers.
I painted belonging.

We called it the General Lee.
Climbed through the windows
like outlaws in cutoff shorts.

I didn't know then what it meant.
Wasn't "woke" enough.
I just knew he let me be wild
and brave
and a little bit reckless.

And funny—
God, he was funny.
He told dirty jokes that made the grown-ups groan
and the kids cackle,
because we only half understood the punchlines.

He'd play along when we told him a rock was a candy bar—
chewed on it like it was the real thing.

We'd punch him in the stomach (not hard),

and he'd pop out his teeth like it was our superpower.

He was strength and silliness wrapped in bibbed overalls.

The kind of grandpa who made you feel tough
but let you laugh with your whole chest.

The kind you didn't realize
you were trying to become
until years later.

TRACK 3.11.G LOVE AND LOSS

Grandpa Belile (or Pops, as I liked to call him.)
He could make you laugh,
even when you weren't sure you should.

On the night before we laid Grandma to rest,
he said:
"I wouldn't have taken a million dollars for her—
but I wouldn't pay ten cents for another one just like her
either."

And somehow,
that seemed like the most honest kind of love I'd ever heard.

When the time came for his funeral a few years later,
He was called—
Preacher.
Governor.
Friend.
Leader.

Jokester.
Patriot.
Strongest man alive.
But Uncle Tom said it best—
"He was the richest poor man I've ever met."
And I knew exactly what he meant.

TRACK 3.11.H BONNETS AND COVERED WAGONS

He was famous in his own right.
Trained a pair of oxen—Mutt and Jeff—
and they pulled a covered wagon through town parades
like something out of a different century.

Holy Smoke and I rode beside them.
Me, in a prairie dress,
bonnet tied tight under my chin.
Waving like I was born to do this.
Like I belonged in that story.

The cheers from the crowd made my ribs hum.
I felt chosen.
Important.
Part of something rooted.
Even if I didn't yet know
what it meant to carry on
a legacy.

I didn't know it at the time,
but they were shaping me—
with puff paint and fishing poles,

with bonnets and black coffee,
with tobacco-stained jokes
and teeth that popped out on command.

They taught me how to be loyal without saying a word,
how to carry pride in the bend of your elbows,
how to hold joy and grief in the same breath.

They showed me that strength could be silent—
or wildly inappropriate.
That love didn't have to be tidy
to be real.
They never sat me down to explain legacy.
They just lived it loud enough
for me to hear it in my bones.

And I've been carrying it ever since—
in my laugh,
in my stubbornness,
in the way I show up
for the people who matter.

I didn't know it then,
but every stolen smoke and mismatched moment—
was a spark.

I was already lighting the way back to myself.

Saints, Shillelaghs & Butterfinger Pie Playlist

"Grandpa (Tell Me 'Bout The Good Old Days)" – The Judds
"Family Tradition" – Hank Williams Jr.

"Coat of Many Colors" – Dolly Parton

Saints, Shillelaghs & Butterfinger Pie Reflection

Who helped raise you—
quietly, imperfectly,
but with a kind of love that still lingers in
your bones?

Think about the grandparents, elders, neighbors, or bonus
relatives who taught you something without a lesson plan.

The ones who didn't always say "I love you," but brewed it into
coffee, tucked it into jokes, or folded it into the laundry.

What is something they gave you—tangible or not—
that you still carry?

And what would it look like to pass it forward—
your own way, in your own time, with your own kind of magic?

Track 4 My Name is Dallas

Some names we're given.
Some we choose.
And some we invent—just to make the world make sense.

In a town of 300 (that was the population in 1978—
now, according to the last census
it has dwindled to just 53.)
Where everybody knows your dog's name
and grandma's famous pie crust recipe—
you'd think I couldn't get away with a lie like that.

But I did.

For a while.

I told the neighbor boys my name was Dallas—
and just like that,
I belonged.

Not because I was trying to trick anyone,
but because Dallas got to do the things I wanted to do.

He climbed trees.
He raced bikes over dirt piles.
He wasn't told, "That's not for girls."

I don't know if I wanted to be a boy
or if I just wanted the freedom they never questioned.

The dust on their jeans.
The calluses on their hands.
There was no second-guessing in them.
No checking themselves before they said yes to adventure.

I played "boys' baseball" because there wasn't a girls' league.
I played second base and pitched.
Made the All-Star team in fifth grade.
Didn't get to play though.
Not because I couldn't play,
but because I was a girl.
And when they remembered that...
I was told to stay home.
Not for lack of skill—
but because I wasn't one of them.

I learned that unfair and talent can sit at the same table,
pretending not to see each other.

I didn't just play boys' baseball.
I rode steers.
At birthday parties,
I would ditch the glitter tables for dirt trails with the brothers.

It wasn't about being a boy.
It was about being free.

Later—
I had lines shaved into the side of my hair
and a permed mullet that spilled down the back of my neck—
through all of junior high.
Before it was cool.
Before TikTok made it trendy.
Before I knew that every buzz of the clippers was my quiet
rebellion.
Trying to shave off what they told me I had to be.

Trying to cut free from the box
they never stopped shoving me into.

What I did know was this—
playing small didn't fit,
and pretending felt easier than being left out.

And those curls in the back?
They weren't just hair.
They were part of me that refused to stay still.

The part that still answered to Dallas
when the world tried to call me anything else.

My Name is Dallas Playlist

"The Joke" – Brandi Carlile
"The Man" – Taylor Swift
"Tomboy" – Destiny Rogers

My Name is Dallas Reflection

Who did you become so you'd be allowed in?
Was it a name?
An attitude?
A quieter version of your light?

What spaces did that version of you get access to?

And what did they have to trade to get there?

Take a moment to honor the version of you that adapted.
Not because they were fake—
but because they were brilliant at survival.

Now ask: Does that version still need to lead?
Or are you ready to take the next swing as yourself?

Track 5 School Daze

This one doesn't play like a single either.
It has its own full playlist.
A collection of moments—
some hilarious, some haunting—
from a girl who learned to speak up for everyone but herself.

I was loud.
But not for me.
I cracked jokes to break tension,
defended classmates from bullies,
made teachers laugh to earn a little space—
and sometimes,
I was the bully.
Not with fists,
but with words that didn't feel like mine
after they landed.

I said what I was told to say.

Did what I thought would make me belong.
And it worked—
until I learned better.

These mini tracks hold the echoes of that silence,
and the reckoning that came with growing up.

This isn't about learning facts.
It's about learning how to come back to your own voice—
when you've used it to protect, perform, and even harm—
and still choose to reclaim it.

TRACK 5.1 GOPHER

When I was five and six,
They called me Gopher.

Not because I dug holes.
Not because I liked tunnels.
But because I'd do whatever the older kids told me to.

I sat in the back of the bus
with the teenagers and the try-hards,
the boys who laughed too loud
and the girls who knew how to weaponize whispering.

They'd feed me lines.
Push me toward their targets.
Make me say things I didn't understand
to people I barely knew.

I was their messenger.

Their dare-taker.
Their wind-up doll.
And I was so proud of it.
At least for a while.

I don't remember the words I said.
But I remember how it felt
to have their attention.

Like I had a role to play.
A spot to fill.
A script to perform
for a seat at their table.

Even if the applause
came at someone else's expense.
Even if that seat
was sticky with power
and shame.

It probably bordered on bullying.
Maybe it was bullying.
I wouldn't have called it that back then.

Back then, I just wanted
to be in.
To be picked.
To matter.
To feel bigger than I was.

Looking back,
I don't feel proud.
I feel protective—

of that little girl
with the too-big backpack
and the too-easy compliance.

I want to sit beside her on that bus
and whisper:
"You don't have to earn your place
by making someone else feel small."

I want to tell her:
It's okay to be kind,
and have boundaries.
It's okay to say no,
even if it means losing the audience.

Because the ones who make you perform
are never the ones who stay.

Gopher Playlist

"Lost Boy" – Ruth B

Gopher Reflection:

Who did you become
in order to be liked?

What part of yourself did you trade
to keep your seat on the bus?

And what would jt look like
to reclaim them now?

TRACK 5.2 SAVE ME A SEAT

When we moved to the farm,
everything changed.

New bus route.
New best friend.

Kevin.

He was eleven years older—
a senior when I was still in grade school.

But he treated me like I mattered.
Like I was worth saving.

Every afternoon,
he'd ask me to save him a seat.

We got released early,
and if Big Bad Sheila got there first—
she'd slam me into the bus wall like it was a sport
and then flip her class ring around,
to thump my skull like I was a drum she owned.

He always came when I needed him.

He taught me how to flip my eyelids inside out
like it was magic.
It kind of was.
A trick that made me laugh
at a time when the world

mostly didn't.

And then one day,
he was gone.

I was at basketball camp.
fifth grade.
Trying to get my layup right.
Trying to belong.

My Mom called.
Her voice sounded like it had been crying long before the
phone rang.

There'd been an accident.
On the farm.
Kevin didn't make it.

The air left the gym
before I left the court.

The world should have stopped.

Instead,
whistles blew.
Balls bounced.
Girls giggled in the hallway.
And I just stood there—
trying to swallow the lump
grief had grown in my throat.

No one else at camp knew who Kevin was.
But I did.

He was the guy who saved me
when grown-ups didn't see me.

The one who taught me how to laugh
on buses that sometimes felt like battlefields.

The one who reminded me
that kindness didn't have to come
with strings or reasons.

Save Me a Seat Playlist

"When I Get Where I'm Going" – Brad Paisley & Dolly Parton
"Angels Among Us" – Alabama

Save Me a Seat Reflection

Who was your Kevin?
The person who showed up when others didn't.
The one who protected you in quiet ways—
with a seat, a smile, a silly trick.

What did they teach you about kindness?

About belonging?

About loss?

If you could say one thing to them now, what would it be?

TRACK 5.3: HIGHWAY TO KINDERGARTEN

On my first day of kindergarten,
I insisted on walking.

Mom had practiced the route with me—
a few trial runs
to make sure I could do it on my own.

When I was barely a block from my house—
I was trapped.
By a bus.
It wouldn't move—just sat there between me and the road I was
supposed to travel.

The driver kept waving at me to hop on.
I kept waving at him
to get the hell out of my way.

He didn't.

I was ready.
I was five
and fierce
and not about to ride a bus
just because it blocked my path.

So I didn't.

I rerouted.

Out onto the highway—
as busy as a highway could be
in a town of 300.

Mom was on the phone with her friend Carla,
telling her I was off to school,
beaming with pride.

Carla glanced out her window and said,
"That's funny—there's a little kid
walking down the highway."

Without missing a beat,
my mom said,
"That has to be Nicole,"
slammed the phone down,
and took off after me.

I wasn't trying to be brave.

I just didn't like being told
there was only one way to get somewhere.

That pattern never really left me.

Even now,
if a path feels too obvious
or too crowded,
I'll make my own.

Not because I'm lost—
but because I know
sometimes the detour

is the real way home.

Highway to Kindergarten Playlist

"Follow Your Arrow" – Kacey Musgraves

Highway to Kindergarten Reflection

Can you remember a time when you took a different route—
literally or metaphorically—
not because it was safer or smarter, but because it felt more
like you?

What did that moment teach you about trust, freedom, or your
own voice?

TRACK 5.4 TEACHER TROUBLE (FEAT. NO FILTER)

When I was in second grade,
I walked right up to the third-grade teacher—
bold, curious, all business.

"Are you going to be my teacher next year?"
She smiled. "Yes, I am."
And I—
with the confidence of a girl who knew the rules of her house—
said,
"Oh great. Now I have to go to a different school because my
mom said there's no way in hell you'll be my teacher."

Dead.
Honest.
Unfiltered.
(Sorry, Mom.)

Was that the gift my grandpa meant
when he said I had something special?

The gift of knowing what to say
without ever checking
if it should be said?

It wasn't a one-time thing.

In preschool Sunday school,
the teacher asked us what to do
if someone tried to attack.
I raised my hand,
and said,
clear as day,
"Kick them in the balls and run like hell."

The teacher—Carla—
was my mom's friend.
The same one my mom had been talking to on the phone
the morning I walked myself down the highway on the first day
of kindergarten.

Carla could barely retell the story,
She was laughing so hard.
When she finally got it out,
my mom just said,
"Well...

that is what I told her."

And maybe that was the gift—
not just a voice that could cut through silence,
but a spirit that refused to be tamed.

Even at four,
I didn't wait for permission to protect myself.
Or to tell the truth.
Or to name what needed naming.
Turns out,
I still don't.

I used to think my voice got me in trouble.
Now I know—it was never the voice that was the problem.

It was a world that wasn't ready
for a girl who didn't wait to be told what to say.

That's the legacy of a girl
raised on instinct,
guts,
and a mom who taught her
to fight smart
and run fast.

Teacher Trouble Playlist

"Brave" – Sara Bareilles

Teacher Trouble Reflection

When was the first time you really said what was on your mind?

Did it get you in trouble—or set you free?

Who taught you how to protect yourself?

And what lessons still live in your voice today?

TRACK 5.5 CLOGS OF JUSTICE

I hated dodgeball.

Especially when we played outside—
lined up like targets
against the brick school wall.

The boys didn't aim.
They launched.
Headshots.
Gut shots.
Bounce-off-the-wall kinds of throws
that made you question your worth
as both a teammate and a human.

And just when you thought it couldn't get worse—
there was Red Rover.

Big boys barreling full speed,
determined to snap our hands in half.

Because what's childhood without
a little mild dislocation?

Every time they yelled,
"Red Rover, Red Rover, send [insert big-tough-guy name here]
right over,"
it was basically a call to arms—
or a call to break them.

And somehow,
they always sent the biggest, meanest kid
charging straight toward the weakest girls in the line.

You'd brace yourself,
locking hands with your best friend like it was a trust-fall—
except no one was catching you.

It wasn't a game.
It was an injury in slow motion.
And you knew
the goal wasn't to win.

It was to smash through and laugh
while your wrist bent backward
and your pride hit the dirt.

But the day I snapped
wasn't during a game.

It was on the swings.
We were just playing.
Just being kids.

And one of the boys pushed Pam.
Hard.
Hit her or knocked her off—
I don't remember exactly.

What I do remember
is the sound of my wooden clogs
hitting the ground
as I charged toward him.

Pam wasn't sweet.
She wasn't fragile.
She was a badass.
Sharp.
Strong.
Tougher than me, for sure.
Cool in ways I only dreamed of being.

The kind of kid who owned her space
without saying a word.

But something about that hit lit a fire.
And by "lit a fire,"
I mean I came at that kid with my wooden clogs
like justice had a size-5 foot and zero chill.

I didn't think.
Didn't hesitate.
I just moved.

Clogs flying,
heart pounding,
justice incoming.

I hated those shoes.
I wanted tennis shoes like the boys
But that day—
they served their purpose.
They became weapons of justice.

I didn't always know how to speak up—
but I knew how to show up.

Even in clunky shoes
and shaky confidence.

Sometimes, your first act of courage
looks like defending someone else.

Clogs of Justice Playlist

"Hit Me With Your Best Shot" – Pat Benatar

Clogs of Justice Reflection

When was the first time you stood up for someone else, and what did it teach you about your own strength?

Have you ever used your "wooden clogs" moment—something you hated—to fight for something that mattered?

TRACK 5.6 FIRST TO SPEAK UP (FEAT. SILENCE & STARTING AGAIN)

By senior year,

I'd learned the power of speaking up.

And the price.

Our basketball coach—
he was...
losing the team.
Clueless.
Inconsistent.
A mess with a whistle.

The whole squad saw it.
Everyone said,
"We've got to say something."

We.
The most dangerous word
when no one means it.

So I did.
I spoke up.

Told the truth.
Straight.
Strong.
Respectful.
Honest.

And when the moment came—
when it was time to back me up—
they didn't.

Not a one.

Just me.

A girl with fire in her chest
and teammates in her shadow.

I quit.

Not out of spite—
but self-respect.

If I couldn't trust the team,
how could I play for it?

But then...
the ache set in.

I missed the game.

The rhythm.

The rush.

The part of me that only woke up
on the court.

So I went back.

Not for the coach.
Not for the girls.
Not for pride.

For love.

For me.

Because even after being left alone,
my voice still mattered.
And so did my joy.

That moment didn't make me bitter.
It made me better.
It taught me how to lead—
with or without the applause.

To speak not for attention,
but from alignment.
And that walking away
can be just as powerful
as walking back in.

First to Speak Up Playlist

"Shake It Out" – Florence + the Machine
"Stronger (What Doesn't Kill You)" – Kelly Clarkson

First to Speak Up Reflection

Have you ever been the first to speak up—
only to be left standing alone?

What did you learn from that silence?

What did you return to—
not because it was easy, but because it was yours?

TRACK 5.7 SLOUGH PISS AND STREET DANCES

High school parties weren't just a thing—
They were an ecosystem.

Gravel pits, lakes, borrowed basements.
Backroads and beer cans.
A rotating cast of truck beds and boomboxes that thumped
Until the big D batteries died.

One time, I was in charge of setup.
We needed a fire pit.
Tires were the go-to fuel—
eco-disaster, teenage treasure.

We found some at the dump
but didn't have a truck.
So I grabbed an old garden hose,
threaded it through the tires,
popped the hatch on the station wagon,
and I rode in back—
arms locked, hose taut,
dragging fire fuel behind us
like some kind of hillbilly parade float.

Another time, at a street dance in Wing,
I decided—
for no reason at all—
to become someone else.

I was my friend's cousin from Tyler, Texas.

Accent and all.

A group of boys from Napoleon gathered 'round,
offering me a Busch Light—
North Dakota's unofficial high school beer.

I waved them off with a laugh:
"Oh no, I can't drink that slough piss.
That's what we call it in Texas."

They cracked up.
Hung on my every word.

I played the part like I was born for it.
And maybe I was.
Even then—
already learning to survive in any space
by becoming whoever the moment required.

Slough Piss and Street Dances Playlist

"Fight for Your Right" – Beastie Boys

Slough Piss and Street Dances Reflection

We learn to shapeshift long before we call it survival.
Sometimes it looks like accents at street dances,
fake names, bold laughs, and party tricks.
Sometimes it looks like loyalty to a moment over a truth.

Who were you pretending to be
when you first started discovering who you were?

And what version of you made people lean in—
even if you weren't sure you belonged?

You don't owe anyone the polished version.
But it's okay to honor the performance
if it helped you find your voice.

TRACK 5.8 MADE-UP BOYFRIENDS

They say imagination is a gift.

But in 5th and 6th grade,
it was my survival strategy.

I made up boyfriends.
Not because I was boy-crazy.

But because I was terrified
someone would look too closely
and see the truth I was trying to outrun.

I gave them names.
Backstories.
Even little love notes.

One of them—
God bless his fictional soul—
even bought me a necklace.
It sparkled just enough to convince people I was normal.

Of course, the whole operation went sideways

the minute I made the mistake of choosing a real person to play
the part.

Rookie mistake.

Word got back to him faster than I could say "rom-com plot
twist," and I was busted.

But the truth is,
I wasn't lying to be cruel.
I was lying to survive.

Because even at ten,
I could feel it—
that pressure to be what everyone expected.

And where I grew up,
girls liked boys.
Period.

So I played the part.
Over and over again.

Why did I do it?
Why did I make up stories,
relationships,
a whole version of myself?

Was it just about hiding?
Or was I trying to prove I could belong in a world that didn't
have room for my truth?

Because it wasn't just about not being found out.

It was about not being left out.

And sometimes, we don't just hide because we're afraid of being hurt—
We hide because we're desperate to be chosen.

Even if we have to disappear a little in the process.

Through junior high, high school, college... and beyond.

I dated a lot.
And I did love a handful of them.

Especially Greg.
He wasn't made up.
He was sweet.
Fun.
Smart.
Sexy.
Safe.

I married him.
Had two amazing sons with him.
We're still good friends—
co-parenting better than most can while married.

And I'll always love him—
for what we had, and for what we let go of with grace.

For who we were,
and how we honored who we became.

So no—not all of the guys I dated were pretend.

But some were placeholders.
Safety valves.
Proof that I was "playing the game" right—
even when my heart was somewhere else entirely.

Some were pages.

Some chapters.
Greg was a whole story.

Made-Up Boyfriends Playlist

"You Learn" – Alanis Morissette

Made-Up Boyfriends Reflection

Have you ever pretended to be someone you weren't—
just to feel safe or accepted?

Is there a moment you look back on now with tenderness for
the version of you who was just trying to belong?

What would it feel like to choose connection without
performance?

TRACK 5.9 SHE-RA

"I'm not hiding who I am anymore."
—She-Ra

They called me She-Ra.

And I didn't know if it was a compliment
or a curse.

It felt like one more reminder
that my body didn't fit
what a girl was supposed to look like.

I wasn't soft.
I wasn't delicate.
I was strong.

Too strong.

At a Future Homemakers of America conference,
a girl glanced at my calves
and said,
"Your legs are so strong."
Her voice was a mix of envy and admiration.

She meant it.
I felt it.

And I've held onto it ever since—
like a flashlight in a dark room.
Because so often,
strength didn't feel like a gift.
It felt like something I had to apologize for.

I wish I'd had different mirrors growing up.
Not just the kind on bathroom walls—
the kind on magazine covers and TV screens.

The kind that reflected women

who looked like me
and loved themselves out loud.

But in the '80s and '90s,
women in sports were mostly invisible.
Less than 5% of televised coverage.
And when they did make it on air,
they were either laughed at
or sexualized.

Turned into jokes.
Or fantasies.

Never equals.
Never heroes.

I needed Venus.
I needed Serena.
I needed P!NK and Ilona
before I had breasts.

Because the breasts came fast.
And they came big.

By fifth grade,
I was shrinking beneath sweatshirts.
Tightening my bra so hard
it left dents in my skin.

I wanted to erase the curves
before anyone noticed them.
But they always noticed.

Pam asked how I got them.
She wanted them.
I didn't.

The only advice I had to offer was from Judy Bloom:
"We must, we must, we must increase our bust."
She laughed.
She believed.
I ached.

I got my period in 4th grade
at a basketball tournament.
Thought I drank too much red Kool-Aid.
Turns out,
my body was just impatient.
It didn't wait for permission.
It just became.
And I hated it for that.

In college,
our friend Becky collected everyone's discarded pizza crusts.
Convinced carbs would fill her bra.

All of us had our rituals.
Our myths.
Our hunger to be wanted
in the right-sized package.

We weren't taught to chase strength.
Only softness.
Only acceptance.

Then came the years of appointments.

Mammograms.
Ultrasounds.
Biopsies.
Probes and paperwork.
By the number four of nine mammograms that year—
I wasn't even nervous anymore.
Just numb.
Same gown.
Same cold room.
Same pain.
Same fear tucked into the corners of my chest.

In 2021, I got a reduction.
Best thing I ever did.

I asked them to take more.
Take all of it.
Free me.

But insurance said:
Not unless you're trans.
Or your family tree is a big red flag.

Because apparently
you need trauma or dysphoria
to qualify for peace.

"I didn't want to be smaller—
I wanted to be stronger.
And now I own that."
—Ilona Maher

And I do too.

Because I'm raising a daughter now.

Her name is Scout—
and she climbs rock walls,
flexes her muscles in the mirror,
and grabs the dumbbells every time I do.

We tell her:
"Be kind, but take no shit."

And we mean it.

Every syllable.

The day she was born,
I called her beautiful.
She gave me side-eye.
That suggested she
did not approve.

So I changed it.
I said,
"Hello, Beautiful Strong."
She nodded.
And she's worn the title like armor ever since.

I don't want her to learn shame in a mirror.

I don't want her hiding her body
or negotiating her worth
or believing that softness equals value.

I want her to see her body

as a compass—
not a cage.

If someone calls her She-Ra,
I hope she grins.
Lifts her chin.
And says,
"Damn right I am."

Because strength was never the problem.
Shame was.

And I don't want to carry that anymore.

Not for her.
And not for me.

Maybe strength starts in the body,
but it grows in the choices we make—
especially the ones we make alone..

She-Ra Playlist

"Just Like a Pill" – Pink
"Scars to Your Beautiful" – Alessia Cara

She-Ra Reflection

What's a compliment you still hold onto like a flashlight?

Were you ever told to hide your strength?

Who benefited from that?

What kind of mirrors did you have growing up?

And what kind are you giving the next generation?

TRACK 5.10 SWING SETS AND SHOOTOUTS

February, 1983.

A man named Gordon Kahl
brought gunfire to Medina.

I didn't know what Posse Comitatus meant.
Still don't, if we're being honest.

But I knew fear when I saw it—
thick and heavy,
sinking into the air like bad weather.

He killed two U.S. Marshals.
Wounded three local officers—
one whose daughter would one day
stand across from me on courts and track fields—
and become my friend.
Both of us already knowing
there were pieces of ourselves
we couldn't quite name yet.

They thought he might be hiding in Heaton,
A tiny town just north of us,

too close for comfort
in a world that was supposed to be small
and safe.

The following night,
we had to perform at the school board meeting.

Sing, dance, pretend we didn't feel
the hush beneath their voices,
or the way the air crackled with what wasn't being said.

After the performance,
they shooed us outside
like it was just another night.

Told us to play.
So we did—
or at least tried to.

I remember the swing set.
The way the chains creaked
against the silence.
The way the sky looked too big,
too empty, too dark.

Every shadow felt like a threat.
Every snap of the wind
a warning shot.

I pumped my legs,
higher, higher—
pretending I wasn't scared
that a man with a stolen cop car

might come tearing through our little playground
and erase us.

He stayed on the run for four months—
but for me,
he never really left.
Some fears don't end
just because the chase does.
They just find a quieter place to hide.

Back then,
this was the closest thing
to a school shooting
I had ever heard of.

We didn't grow up
practicing lockdown drills
or bulletproof backpacks.

We grew up with shotguns
hanging proud in the back windows
of beat-up trucks during deer season—
Nobody is thinking twice about it.

Guns weren't the fear.
Not then.
The fear was the crack in the world,
how it could split wide open
on an ordinary night,
and no one could tell you
if it would ever close again.

Swing Sets and Shootouts Playlist

"In the Air Tonight" – Phil Collins

Swing Sets and Shootouts Reflection

Think back— was there a moment you first realized
the world wasn't as safe
or simple
as you'd been told?

Where were you?
What were you doing?
What did it change?

TRACK 5.11 SICK DAYS AND SHOWCASE SHOWDOWNS

If I got sick at school,
they didn't haul me twelve miles home.
I got to go to Grandma's.

Grandma and Grandpa lived
0.3 miles from school—
close enough to hear teachers yelling at us to come inside from
recess
if the wind blew just right.

The second the office called,
Grandma would climb onto her stool
by the big picture window,

watching the road
like a lighthouse keeper,
waiting for me to come into view.

Sick days were simple back then.
No urgent cares.
No WebMD spirals.
Just a couch with crocheted afghans,
a sleeve of saltine crackers,
a glass of 7Up with three ice cubes,
and The Price is Right on TV.

The smell of coffee always lingered in the air,
even if she wasn't drinking it.

The house was warm but never loud—
except when the grandfather clock struck the hour,
booming like it had something important to say.

I'd sink into the cushions,
drift between dreams and doorbells,
guessing the price of microwaves
and living room sets
like it was serious business.

Some days I was too tired to guess,
just listening to the clapping,
the spinning wheels,
the voices calling out dollar amounts
like tiny wishes.

When you're little,
the world feels enormous.

But a living room with a handmade quilt,
a cold soda,
and Bob Barker telling you to "come on down"—
it was enough to make you feel
like you'd already won something.

Sick Days and Showcase Showdowns Playlist

"Grandma's Hands" – Meg Mac

Sick Days and Showcase Showdowns Reflection

Who was your "lighthouse"?

Who watched for you—
even when you didn't know you needed watching?

Where were you safe enough to be small,
sick,
sleepy,
and still feel like you belonged?

TRACK 5.12 REPORT CARDS & RULE BREAKERS (FEAT. SCRATCH-AND-SNIFF & SIDELINE SHAME)

In third grade,
I didn't like sitting at my desk.

So I sat under it.

Every day.

No real reason—
I just felt better down there.
Cozy. Safe.
Like the world made more sense
from below.

My teacher didn't yell.
Didn't send me to the hall.
She gave me stickers.
Every day I sat in my seat—
properly—
I got one.

Scratch-and-sniff.
Grape. Root beer.
Pizza, even. (Why though?)

Eventually,
I earned a whole collection.

A tiny museum of compliance
pressed against the top of my desk.

Positive reinforcement, they called it.
Conditioning,
if we're being clinical.

But it worked.
I sat.
Earned my scents.
I learned the right way to show up.

Even if I didn't understand why.

By fifth grade,
I wasn't under desks anymore.
But I was under pressure.

We didn't just play sports.
We earned them.
My mom had a rule:
No C or better?
No game.

I had a D.
Not on my report card—
not yet.
Just a midterm grade
caught red-handed
by a parent who meant what she said.

So I suited up—
in regular clothes.
Sat at the end of the bench
like I was academically ineligible,
like my jersey had been revoked
by the invisible hand of maternal justice.

I still remember the sting.
Not from missing the game—
but from feeling seen
in the worst way.

Benched by a grade.
Grounded by a rule.

Reminded that effort wasn't just about hustle—
it was also about homework.

I got the grade up.
Played the next game.
But I never forgot that feeling.
Of being present
but not playing.
Of being so close to belonging,
but stuck in the wrong uniform.

Report Cards & Rule Breakers Playlist

"Don't Let Me Get Me" – P!NK

Report Cards & Rule Breakers Reflection

Where were you first taught that rules mattered more than
reasons?

What "sticker system" shaped how you showed up?

And were you ever benched—
not for who you were, but for how you didn't measure up... yet?

TRACK 5.13 RIVERS AND REVELATIONS

In 7th and 8th grade,
our science club packed up and headed northeast, canoeing
down the Crow Wing River in Minnesota.

It was the best kind of adventure.
The kind you didn't realize
was stitching itself into you
until years later.

Each morning,
we packed everything we had—
clothes, camping gear, food—
crammed into canoes,
and shoved off.

By night,
we'd pull over wherever the river whispered yes—
clear out a patch of woods,
and pitch tents under the stars.

Each day,
we switched canoe partners—
a new rhythm to figure out,
a new battle with the river.

One day,
I got paired with Buzz.
All he wanted to do was fish—
reel in something big,
while the current did all the actual work.

It wasn't so bad
when the river carried us.
We drifted along well enough,
lazy and laughing.

But when we hit a lake,

and the water turned flat and stubborn—
and there was no current to hide behind—
I couldn't take it anymore.

After a while,
I gave up trying to do both the steering
and the paddling.
Jumped into the water,
and let the water hold me instead.

I saw things on that trip
I'd only ever heard about at home.
Eel-like fish sliding through the shallows,
great blue herons lifting like shadows off the water,
giant turtles digging slow, careful nests in the sand.
Even the eagles looked bigger out there—
heavier, somehow,
like they carried the weight of the whole sky.

At night, the older boys got restless.
One year, a couple of them said
they were going to hike into town—
find a bar,
since the drinking age in Minnesota was only nineteen.

I don't know if they ever actually made it,
and honestly,
I don't even think they were nineteen either.

Someone had brought a Ouija board,
because of course they did.

We spent nights half-scared, half-laughing,

asking questions we weren't old enough to understand,
pretending not to shove the pointer ourselves.

One night,
we asked if our teacher's dog
was going to jump out of the canoe.
The board said yes.

The next day,
the dog leapt right into the river—
proving once and for all
that maybe we weren't the only ones
the river was talking to.

I loved those trips more than anything.
The woods, the water,
the way life stretched wider
than school walls and small-town maps.

Even back then,
before I really knew who I was
or where life would take me,
I knew one thing for sure:
I wanted to come back someday,
with kids of my own.

Let them paddle and drift and dream,
just like I did.

We finally made it happen—
the same river,
maybe even the same canoes,
with the same wild-hearted feeling.

We used the same outfitter too—
Gloege's—
still sending new dreamers down the same old currents.

The story for that trip is waiting,
just around the next bend.

Rivers and Revelations Playlist

"Wide Open Spaces" The Chicks

Rivers and Revelations Reflection

When did you first taste real freedom—
not the kind someone hands you,
but the kind you find on your own?

What was your Crow Wing River—
that first place that felt bigger, wilder, and more possible than
you ever knew to dream?

TRACK 5.14 HEY NIKKI

I played JV basketball in 6th grade,
varsity by 7th.

I loved that sport.
The sound the ball makes when
it hits the floor,
the sharp squeak of sneakers,
the way a good pass felt

like a secret you could throw.

I started varsity track in 6th grade too.

Small schools need numbers—
but I was good.

Small-town good.

The kind of good
where your name makes the weekly paper,
and half the bleachers already know your stats by heart.

Where the lunch lady slips you an extra cookie
because you broke the shot put record on Tuesday.

I wasn't a runner,
but sometimes they needed extra points—
so they'd toss me into the 1600 or 3200 meter relay,
legs burning, lungs on fire,
dragging a thrower's body down the track
like it owed me something.

I ran
because they asked.
I ran
because I could.
I ran
because sometimes
moving forward
was the only way
to not look back.

My track coach, Mr. K—
Big Daddy, we called him—
believed in me before I even knew
what that could mean.

He saw something.
Even when I couldn't.
Even when the version of me showing up to practice
was half-tired, half-numb,
and all the way pretending to be okay.

He was also my shop teacher.
I built a hope chest in that class—
still full of high school memories.
The good ones, of course.
I built a curio cabinet.
And a lamp that looked like a well.
Because part of me already knew
I'd need something to hold light someday.

He taught me how to drive,
white-knuckling our way
to hockey games and bowling in neighboring towns.

And then there was the Green Bomb.
I don't even know what kind of car it was—
maybe an old hearse—
but we'd pile ten of us into that thing
like it was a clown car from the underworld.
He'd drop us off a few miles out of town
on a gravel road and make us run home.

He took Buzz and me to track meets all over,

even out of state sometimes,
rolling down endless highways,
eating gas station snacks,
chasing better times and longer throws.

It wasn't just about the medals.
He knew
what it meant
to be seen.
He handed me a shot put
like it was a crown.

I qualified for state
my eighth-grade year—
the first, last and only time I would.

Big Daddy left after that season—
and I think a part of my confidence
drove off with him.

He used to sing "Hey Nikki"
to the tune of Toni Basil's "Hey Mickey,"
clapping off-beat,
making me laugh
like it was my own private anthem.

He had no idea
what was happening under the stairs
outside the history room.

But for a little while,
he made me believe
I was stronger than the silence.

And for a girl
who hadn't yet learned
how to speak her story—
that belief
was everything.

Hey Nikki Playlist

"Hey Mickey" – Toni Basil

Hey Nikki Reflection

When did you first realize your strength—
not just the kind measured by medals or trophies,
but the kind that carried you through things no one else
could see?

TRACK 5.15 FROM BUMBLEBEES TO BIG DREAMS

There were eight of us in kindergarten.
At our graduation,
we sang "Bringing Home a Baby Bumblebee"
and "My Cousin Paul Has a Basketball."

We made boutonnières out of Kleenex,
the edges carefully tipped with green marker
to match our school colors—
tissue flowers pinned proudly
to our Sunday best.

The songs were silly,
the day was sticky with paper cups of punch and excitement,
and none of us had any idea
how much growing up there was still left to do.

By high school graduation,
the world had gotten bigger,
but our class did not.

Fred—our token male—
stood out among the cap-and-gown ponytails and hairspray.

At our ceremony,
we sang "One Moment in Time,"
our voices stretching toward something
we couldn't quite see yet.

There were so few of us,
all four graduates got to speak.

It only took twenty minutes—
short enough that a year later in college,
a group of us got written up for a noise violation
watching the VHS tape in my dorm room,
laughing too loud at our awkward speeches and earnest tears.

I don't know for sure,
but I'm pretty confident
I graduated in the bottom half of my class—
with a 3.8 GPA.

My senior math class was even smaller.
Only me.

At the end of the year,
my teacher left a note:
"To my favorite student in Senior Math."
They say teachers aren't supposed to have favorites,
but sometimes,
it's safe to say the obvious.

From baby bumblebees and basketball songs,
to bus trips and offbeat anthems,

School Daze stitched itself into me—
loud and soft,
crooked and proud.

It wasn't perfect.
It was patched together with
Kleenex flowers, silly songs,
paper awards, and whispered dreams.

But somehow,
it was enough
to stitch a heart strong enough
to keep beating.

School taught me how to
diagram a sentence.
But life taught me how to finish one—
with my own voice.

From Bumblebees to Big Dreams Playlist

"Baby Bumblebee" – Cedarmont Kids

"One Moment in Time" – Whitney Houston

From Bumblebees to Big Dreams Reflection

What stitched you together when you didn't even realize it?
The songs you sang off-key.
The friends who filled the empty seats.

DISC TWO:
Break the Silence

DISC TWO: Break the Silence

Silence only works until it doesn't.
It's a shelter
until it starts to feel like a cage.
When the words start leaking through
the cracks you built for safety.

For years, the safest thing I could do
was stay quiet—
hold it in, hold it together,
hold my breath and hope it passed.

Disc Two is where mine began to slip out—
not because I was ready,
but because staying silent was costing more
than speaking ever could.

This is where the noise begins,
and the truth, too.
This is where the healing learns my name.

DISC TWO Playlist

"Surface Pressure" – Jessica Darrow

Track 6 ITSNIK Is Here

My license plate read ITSNIK—
not because I needed everyone to know who I was,
but because I needed me
to know.

A subtle announcement. A quiet claim.
It said: I'm here.
Even if I didn't fully know who that was yet.

It was a reminder that I was someone.
Someone who showed up.
Someone who could belong somewhere, eventually.

We rolled into Mitchell, South Dakota
in the middle of the night—
with a road-trip headache, a trunk full of Target bins,
and the two women I loved
who drove me across state lines
and then vanished before I'd even finished unpacking.

I remember pulling into the parking lot of the hotel,
and there it was—
a note taped to the door,
the key to our room dangling underneath it.

They had already gone home.
No late-night check-ins back then.
Just a note, a key, and a motel door that didn't latch quite right.

It wasn't cold, but something about the air felt sharp.
The town was quiet—
The kind of quiet that either comforts you
or calls your bluff.

I'd move into the dorms the next day.
But that night?
It felt like I was already on my own.

There were only three of us from North Dakota
there that year.
It felt far—like I'd landed in someone else's story,
where the laundry cost 75 cents a load
and no one knew my name yet.

But I didn't flinch.
I just started figuring it out.

A stranger's dad helped build my loft—
thanks to my mom, who met him in the lumber aisle at
Menards
and recruited him on the spot.
With him came his daughter Teresa—
bubbly, bright,

and just a little too perky for my taste at the time.

She showed up uninvited
and immediately started flipping through my cassette tapes
like she lived there.

She and her twin sister were cheerleaders.
I was a jock.
Different ecosystems,
same planet.

Somehow it worked.
We became lifelong best friends,
even if she entered my life like a full-blown halftime show.

That first day,
all the other parents stayed for the goodbye ceremony.
Mom and Dorleen didn't—
They had a long drive back.

So I sat alone in Hugh's Building—
the old science hall theater—
watching a mime troupe perform a strange interpretive mantra:

"Listen to your thoughts.
Listen to your feelings.
Listen. Listen."

It was weird.
And yet... profound.

Those words still echo when I'm quiet enough.

I think they were acting out potential college scenarios—
academic pressure, roommate drama, identity quests wrapped
in body paint.

No dialogue besides that repeated mantra.
Just exaggerated movement,
white masks to cover their faces,
and the unmistakable message,
before the professors, the parties, the existential panic—
that the real curriculum was inside.

That same stage would later host me—
hypnotized in front of half the college,
playing a Martian interpreter
with way too much enthusiasm.

Later I would act in and direct plays there too.
That stage knew more versions of me
than most people ever did.

That room would eventually be renamed the Patten-Wing
Theatre,
after one of my favorite professors—
the theater director who taught me communication,
connection,
and even Japanese.

Eventually, the building was condemned.
But on that day
it held something sacred—
a strange, silent invitation
to start listening
in a whole new way.

My roommate was a year older—
funny, quick,
a faithful servant of God.

A basketball player, just like me—
at least for a little while.
She taught me how to work the washing machines
and where to find the good cereal in the dining hall.

She was also neat.
I... was not so much.
She hated that I would leave dirty silverware laying around,
so one time I hid it from her—
in her underwear drawer.
We laugh about that—
now.

One night we talked the Domino's crew
into letting us make our own pizzas—
but only if we ate an anchovy first.
We did.
It was awful.
Totally worth it.

She was also biracial.
And while that didn't matter to me,
it mattered that I noticed it—
because outside of Coach Cy at basketball camp,
I hadn't had real conversations with anyone who wasn't white.

I didn't realize how small my world had been
until it quietly started expanding.

Her sister was on the volleyball team.
Later, we'd play softball together.

Their mom made the best homemade egg rolls I'd ever had—
the kind you remember for life
because they were served with laughter, love,
hot oil, and zero measuring cups.

We became fast friends.
Years later, we won the roommate game—
like the newlywed game,
but with inside jokes instead of kissing.

I don't know exactly what drew me to that school.
Well—maybe I do.

A fiery admissions rep
from a small North Dakota town
in my own backyard.

She chased me down with brochures
and yearbook pictures of handsome boys I would meet.
That part didn't do much for me.
But her energy? That stuck.
So did the promise of a place I could plug into,
where I could be seen, involved, maybe even needed.

And plug in—I did!.
Hard.

I played basketball—
until I got too sick, too tired,
and realized I was just small-town good.

I was on the track team for a season—
same thing.
Decent for a district of dirt road
and homemade trophies.

I played second base
on the very first softball team.
Held my own.
Started game after game.

Then one game, chaos hit.
Our catcher—
my roommate's sister—
got kicked out for kicking dirt at the ump.
(It was justified, for the record.)

Before I could even process what happened,
Coach shoved a chest protector at me
and said, "You're up."

The gear didn't fit,
the mask was hanging sideways,
and I had approximately three seconds
to figure out how to squat like a catcher,
and send the pitcher a sign.

But somehow, I did it.
Because that's what college ball—and life—taught me early:
sometimes you don't get a heads-up,
you just get handed the gear and go.

I acted.
Directed.

Led the Human Services Club.
Served on the Student Council.

I partied with the wild kids.
Prayed with the church crew.
Studied with the scholars.

If it had a sign-up sheet,
My name was probably on it.

Each one was a mirror—
and I learned how to bend the light just right.

I was everywhere.

A college chameleon.
Able to blend in with just about anyone—
the athletes, the artists, the introverts, the evangelicals.

Each group saw a piece of me,
but none of them saw the whole.

I got along with everyone.
Was it because I was trying to fit in—
or because I genuinely loved them all?
Maybe both.

Maybe that's what made me so easy to be around—
and so easy to overlook.

And maybe that's what college is for:
learning how to shape-shift without disappearing.

I wasn't lost.
But I wasn't fully found either.

Becoming isn't loud at first.
Sometimes it starts with a license plate
and a room full of strangers.

Fast forward to senior year—
I'd be on the homecoming court,
and a Miss Wesleyan finalist.

That title sounded like a pageant,
but it wasn't about tiaras.
It was about
Leadership, service, character,
a GPA above 3.25
and a resume packed tighter than a dorm fridge after your mom
visits.

Interviews. Committees.
A banquet with real linens.
It was the kind of honor that made your parents cry
and your professors nod with quiet pride.

Miss Wesleyan dated back to 1929—
long before I ever walked those halls.
And that year,
I stood among the finalists.

Me.
The chameleon.

Maybe all that shape-shifting
wasn't about disappearing after all.

Maybe it was about becoming
someone worth seeing.

ITSNIK Is Here Playlist

"Cool Kids" – Echosmith
"Vienna" – Billy Joel

ITSNIK Is Here Reflection

You don't always know when becoming begins.
Sometimes, it doesn't look like a grand entrance.
It looks like hauling Target bins into a dorm room
and watching your cassette tapes get rifled through by a
stranger.

It looks like trying on different friend groups
until one of them finally feels like a fit.

Think back to your own "firsts"—
not just when you arrived somewhere new,
but when you started becoming someone new.

Who were you before the world told you who to be?

Where did you first start shape-shifting?

What pieces of you got lost in the blending in?

Which ones are you ready to reclaim?

Write it down. Speak it out loud.
Or simply say: I'm still here. And I'm still becoming.

Track 7 Skool Daze:
Next Level (mini tracks)

College wasn't just a campus—
it was a collision.
Of who I thought I was
and who I was becoming.

A place where late-night study sessions turned into therapy,
and syllabi couldn't keep up with life lessons.
Where I learned to lead without permission,
love without a manual,
and live on caffeine, faith,
and whatever hope I could stuff into a backpack with borrowed
textbooks.

This track isn't about GPA or graduation—
it's about growth.
The kind that happens between heartbreak and hustle,
between knowing it all
and realizing you don't.

These are the mini tracks
from the next level of my Skool Daze—
where education met evolution,
and the real major was becoming me.

TRACK 7.1 ARMS IN THE BACKSEAT (JC & CO)

I was always told God loved me
(He loves all the little children, right?!)
But there were always the sermons
that suggested maybe they only meant
the acceptable parts of me.

Still, I believed in God.
Even when I hadn't quite figured out
what I believed about myself.

I joined JC & Co—
Jesus Christ and Company.

We were part choir, part storyteller troupe,
part living altar call on wheels.

We sang.
We moved like the music was calling us home.
We shared stories.
We traveled to churches across the Midwest,
a couple vans full of faith and props,
and the kind of idealism only young adults can carry without
breaking.

Every third Sunday or so brought a new sanctuary—
tight harmonies,
interpretive dance,
and testimonies in borrowed pulpits.

And I loved it.
Maybe it was the performing.
Maybe it was the people.
Maybe it was God.
Maybe it was the first space
where my heart felt louder than my fear.

When we visited my home church,
I got to give the testimonial.
I don't remember what I said—
but I remember what it felt like:
a full-circle kind of grace.

Sometimes they clapped.
Sometimes they cried.
Sometimes they just stared.

But the moment I really remember—
the one that changed me—
wasn't in a church.

It was in the backseat of a car,
headed to a ski retreat in the Black Hills.
Laura and Kris up front,
me quiet in the back—
the highway blurred.

And suddenly—

I felt it.

Not the idea of God.
Not the rulebook version.
Not the voice of someone else's Bible.

I felt arms.
Warm.
Wrapped.
Real.

A presence that didn't just love me—
it knew me.
All of me.
Even the parts the world said were wrong.
Even the silence I kept
about who I might be becoming.

It felt like being held
by something that had always been there—
but I was finally still enough to feel it.

And even now—
when I see the posts,
the pulpit clips,
the performances—
trying to say otherwise—

I remember that night.

And I know what I felt was real.

It didn't say, "You're wrong."

It said, "You're mine."
All of you.

And I still believe that.
Even when the world forgets how to love like that—

I remember.

Arms in the Backseat (JC & Co) Playlist

"Known" – Tauren Wells
"Awesome God" – Rich Mullins
We sang this one at almost every performance—
hands lifted, hearts on fire,
belting out that our God wasn't just good—
He was awesome.

It wasn't just a song.
It was our anchor.
Our declaration.
Our troupe anthem.
Declaring a God big enough to hold
all our contradictions.

Arms in the Backseat (JC & Co) Reflection:

Have you ever felt the presence of love before words could
explain it?

Where were you?

What did your body know that your mind hadn't caught up

to yet?

Who or what told you you didn't belong—
and can you offer that part of you a new story?

Write the version of God (or Love, or Truth) you wish had been
spoken over you as a teen.

Then read it out loud to your younger self.

TRACK 7.2 BULLDOG & THE BRAIN CELLS

I partied in college—
much like high school—
hard and fast
unless it was "in season" for sports.
Even my brain cells and liver got scheduled rest days.

The first party I went to,
I thought I'd make an entrance.
A vintage Taco John's cup—20 oz—
half full of 3 Wise Men:
Jack Daniels, Jim Beam, Johnnie Walker.

I said I'd drink it in one go.
Smile after.
People tossed dollars on the table
like I had a pole to swing from.

I did it.
Guzzled the whole thing.

Smiled like a champ.
And then—
puked all night in the bushes.
But hey—
I got their dollars.

At parties,
I was part choreographer, part jukebox.
Chumbawamba. Proclaimers. Ace of Base.
I didn't just dance—
I performed.
(The world was my stage.)

When I got knocked down, I didn't just get back up—
I did clap push-ups to Chumbawanba
like a one-woman pep rally
before I got back up again.
I stirred up a crowd before I even knew what
"hype-woman" meant.

I'd turn a kitchen into a concert hall,
grab a butter knife—instant mic—
and belt out What's Up like it was my anthem.

500 Miles?
That's not just a song.
It's a theme song—
For one of my core group of friends.
We still belt it out—
off-key, full-volume, no shame.

My summer co-ed softball team nicknamed me Bulldog
because I drank Colorado Bulldogs.

Before I was Bulldog,
before the dorms, the push-up parties, and the jukebox nights—
there was McQuade's.

The summer before college,
at McQuade's—
the world's largest slow-pitch softball tournament—
I played on a Canadian men's team
I'd met the night before
at a place called The Broken Oar.

I wasn't supposed to be there to play.
Just came to watch.
But the universe, some beers, and their shortstop had other
plans.

I had to borrow their shoes.
They didn't really fit.
But somehow—
I did.

One year, our co-ed team headed to the state softball tournament in Pierre.
I was drunk in the backseat, trying to give my mom directions
over the phone.

The team kept saying we were playing at "Oahe"—
the name of the softball complex.

But my drunk ears kept hearing Hawaii.

So there I was, yelling into the phone,
"These assholes keep saying Hawaii,

but I know the tournament's in Pierre!"

My mom just laughed and said,
"I'll get to town and figure it out."

I was also the fastest beer guzzler in Davison County.

A human funnel.
I could take a can of beer like it was water hitting concrete.

One night, I was out with my coach/team sponsor,
and his men's team was getting destroyed
in a guzzling contest at the Jackpot.
Coach stood up and said,
"But can you beat Bulldog?"

The rules:
Pitcher of beer on your head.
Drink it.
Put it back upside down on your head when done.
By the time he took his first sip, I was already getting a standing
ovation.
Cheers all around.
I think they even sang "For She's a Jolly Good Fellow."

I also crushed beer cans on my forehead.
(Zero stars. Do not recommend.)

And there was the night of the "straight tequila" meltdown—
spiraling after a C on my report card.

Only to realize Monday morning
there was no way I earned a C.

I tracked every assignment.
I knew my math.

Back then, grades were typed in manually—
no internet, no fancy portals,
just fingers, forms, and a hope you didn't hit the wrong line.

So I marched into his office,
hungover but righteous,
grade calculations in hand.

Sure enough—
he'd entered someone else's score.

Grade: fixed.
Report card: redeemed.
Dignity?
Still fuzzy.

We always got hungry after partying.
That usually meant a trip to the I-90 truck stop
for hash browns and gravy,
a gas station Chuckwagon sandwich nuked into oblivion,
or—on our most chaotic nights—
a run to the grocery store.

But we couldn't make decisions to save our lives.

So we brought a die.
Each number stood for a snack.
Roll a 3? Cheese puffs.
Roll a 5? Berry Pop-Tarts.
Roll a 6? It's a free-for-all.

Not that we ever stuck to the roll.
But hey—it felt like structure.

I never touched drugs—
terrified and always said
"Do drugs and die."

If drugs showed up, I left.
Until senior year.
They sold me on weed like it was a miracle cure.
"Medicinal. Natural. Safe."

I tried.
I didn't feel anything.
I tried harder.

Eventually, I asked to be taken back to the dorms.
(Which, by the way, I loved—
I lived in the dorms all four years.
If adulthood didn't require bills and boundaries,
I'd still be living in one now.
There was always someone to talk to,
something going on,
a hallway full of backup plans.)

Once there,
I started puking—
alcohol and weed apparently don't make a great cocktail.

Then I thought a shower might help.
But mid-rinse,
it hit—
like a black curtain closing over my eyes.

Next thing I knew,
I was waking up on the nasty dorm shower floor,
soaked, disoriented,
and very clear on one thing:
I went right back to believing
"if I do drugs, I die."

It wasn't my proudest moment,
but it was one I never forgot.

I wouldn't relive all of these moments...
but I wouldn't erase them either.

They were wild.
Messy.
Half-glorious, half-regrettable.
And somehow, still mine.

The stories?
They never really leave.
They just wait
for the right song to come on.

Bulldog & the Brain Cells Playlist

"Tubthumping" – Chumbawamba
"Closing Time" – Semisonic
"Good Riddance (Time of Your Life)" – Green Day
"Straight Tequila Night" – John Anderson

Bulldog & the Brain Cells Reflection

What's a story from your past
you used to feel ashamed of...
but now see as a sign you were just trying to belong, survive,
or feel something real?

Where were you reckless,
and what were you really reaching for?

What parts of those wild nights still live in you today—
and what have they taught you about power, presence,
or letting go?

TRACK 7.3 THE TAPE NEVER LIES

In college,
you rarely saw me without a big ol' VHS camera strapped to
my shoulder.
Everything was on tape—
the parties, the pranks,
the dorm-room chaos,
karaoke sessions,
and impromptu theater.

One trip to Bismarck,
visiting my high school bestie Chas at UMary,
I took it to the next level.
I pretended to be a reporter from KFYR-TV.

With a few friends in on the joke,
I stormed the athletes' dorms—

microphone in hand (yes, it was fake),
asking the hard-hitting questions:
How's the transition to college sports life?

Some were already asleep—
but they still sat up, rubbed their eyes,
and answered like pros.

One girl?
She went full SNL Gap Girl on me—
big hair, big attitude,
and the kind of charisma that makes you say,
She's gonna be somebody someday.

Spoiler: She's now a professional sports announcer.
I'm still convinced my "exclusive interview" was her unofficial
debut.
I really do need to get those tapes transferred to digital.

A couple years ago, a few friends and I dusted off a VHS
player,
gathered in an Airbnb,
and hit play.

The off-key performance of What's Up?
Yeah, it made the cut.
It always makes the cut.

We laughed at our hair, our outfits, our confidence—
but underneath it all, there was a tenderness too.
A kind of recognition:
Oh...she was already becoming something.
Even then.

Even before I had a camera in my hands,
I was finding ways to tell a story.
I'd walk around, reciting poetry—
but not the kind from a textbook.

These were song lyrics, spoken like verses,
because that's what felt real.

It started in high school,
when the teacher wouldn't let me read Horton Hears a Who.
She said it was too rhymey.
So I stood up and delivered Every Rose Has Its Thorn—
line by line,
trying to keep a straight face and not sing,
while my classmates tried not to crack up.

Another one of my greatest hits?
Life's a Dance—you learn as you go.

I didn't just read the words.
I lived them.

Maybe it started in those college days,
with the impromptu concerts, video interviews,
and the songs I turned into poetry.
I was already practicing the art of saying things that mattered—
in the best way I knew how.

I didn't know it then,
but one day, those words would become promises.
One day, I'd stand in front of the woman I love and say—
Today and always, I cross my heart and promise to...
...and the rest, well...

that story is still being written.

Looking back now,
it's funny—
I wasn't just playing a reporter,
or a performer,
or a storyteller.
I was one.

Long before I had a title,
before I called it a job,
I was already gathering stories,
capturing the magic of the moment,
making people feel seen.

It's all there—
in those tapes,
in the skits and songs,
in the questions I asked,
and the way I listened.

Those tapes weren't just silly moments caught on camera.
They were proof—
proof that I was always a storyteller,
a collector of moments,
a girl who found joy in helping other people feel seen, heard,
and part of the show.

I thought I was just goofing around,
but I was learning how to hold the mic for others,
how to capture the feeling of a room,
how to make something ordinary feel extra.

And maybe that's the real magic—
in the way those moments shaped me into someone who still
loves to ask the questions,
shine a light on the small,
and tell the stories that make us feel alive.
Every grainy frame was a breadcrumb
leading me to the work I do now.

And let me tell you about full-circle moments—
they find you.

Fast forward twenty years—
there I was, standing on a stage,
lip-syncing my heart out to What's Up by 4 Non Blondes,
and winning a trip to Jamaica.

Same song.
Same spirit.
Just a bigger audience.
Still a girl with a mic (or maybe a butter knife).
Still telling the story.

The Tape Never Lies Playlist

"What's Up" – 4 Non Blondes
"Every Rose Has Its Thorn" – Poison
"Life's a Dance" – John Michael Montgomery

The Tape Never Lies Reflection

What moments in your life felt like "just for fun"—
but looking back, you see they were actually defining you?

What songs take you right back—
to a dorm room, a dance floor, a driveway concert with your
best friends—
where you didn't just sing along, you became the song?

When was the last time you looked at an old photo,
a dusty home video,
or even a random voice memo on your phone—
and realized you were watching yourself become who you are
today?

Take a moment to remember.
Replay the tape.
What story were you already telling,
long before you had a title for it?

TRACK 7.4 DEGREES THAT FOUND ME

I never declared them,
not in the formal
"this is my major"
kind of way.

I think they declared me.
I just kept signing up for what made me curious—
what felt human, what felt real.
By junior year,
Pam Boline—
my advisor, my anchor—
sat me down and said,
"Let's make this make sense."
And we did.

I didn't know what I was building back then.
But Pam did.
She believed in me before I even had language for myself.
She saw order in the chaos I called curiosity.
And made me feel like my way of learning wasn't wrong—
it was just different.

I graduated with degrees in Human Services and Behavioral
Science,
with concentrations in Psychology and Criminal Justice.

Two credits short of a communications minor—
until the head of the department gifted me those missing
pieces,
handed me an A,
and sealed it with a wink,
as repayment for all the speech competitions I judged during
college.

I still don't really know how it all happened.
Maybe I was just...following the thread.

I started out wanting to tape ankles.
Athletic training sounded cool
until they handed me a science schedule
thicker than a dictionary.

"No thanks," I said,
and pivoted without looking back.

Even then, biology clung to me.
I took it not once,
but twice—

not because I failed,
but because I chose to take it
credit/no credit
to protect my GPA.
First time: C-
Which, in that system, meant
"Do it again."
And I did.

Funny thing is,
I could tutor biology.
And I did.
I helped the football team
during study tables.

I coached classmates through photosynthesis,
cellular respiration,
the parts of the brain—
but memorization and regurgitation?
That wasn't my game.
I needed to feel it to remember it.

I wasn't just studying.
I was doing.
I was a night advocate
at the domestic violence shelter.

I was a mentor
for the Wrap Around Project:
one more misstep,
and those kids were getting sent away.
I tried to meet them before the system did.

I interned at a juvenile prison,
then stayed on as emergency staff—
cottage duty,
watching,
listening,
learning how cycles start
and how rarely they break.

Somehow,
by the time I graduated,
I had more real-world experience
than people twice my age.

Experience doesn't always come with salary or status—
sometimes it comes with sleepless nights
and stories you never stop carrying.

That's how I became
one of the youngest child protection workers in state history.
Not because I had the perfect GPA,
but because I had already been in the rooms.

Already held the stories.
Already knew the weight of systems built for survival,
not healing.

It wasn't the plan.
But it was the path.
And it led me straight into the work
my heart already knew how to do.

Graduation kind of snuck up on me.
One week I was juggling finals

and the next, I was supposed to know
what I wanted to be when I grew up.

Spoiler: I didn't.
Not really.
I flirted with the idea of becoming a school counselor.
It felt practical. Predictable. Safe.

But life had other plans—and I wasn't one to sit still.
I took a job as a program coordinator
at a Boys & Girls Club.
Just a few months.
Just long enough to realize
I was meant to be deeper in the story.

That's how I found myself
working in child protection.
Not playing referee—
but showing up at the moment
when the story split
and helping kids live the version where they made it.

The work was heavy—
not just in theory,
but in your soul.

It wasn't a promotion.
It was a baptism.

I carried stories
that still haunt me sometimes.
I did the best I could
in a system that wasn't built for softness.

But then
my Grandpa died.
And not long after,
My Sister's boyfriend was killed in a motorcycle accident.

After six years of living in South Dakota—
after burnout and breakthroughs,
grit and grief—
It was time to move back.

The grief was layered.
It clung to everything.
I needed proximity to my people—
not just emotionally,
but geographically.

So I moved back to North Dakota.
Back to the flat, honest sky
and the rhythm of family.

I worked in higher ed for a while—
admissions and financial aid.
Helping students start their journeys
while still piecing together my own.

One year into that role,
one of the kids I had worked with in child protection
stopped by to visit.

I gave her a tour of the campus.
We walked past the brick buildings,
talked about classes,
life,

possibility.

Then she looked at me—
a little older,
a lot wiser—
and said,
"So, this is what you do now?"

I nodded.
"Yep."

She paused.
Then said it again—
but this time, like a gut punch truth:
"Kids like me need you. And this is what you do?"

That line settled in my bones.
Not as shame—
but as a reminder.
Not of failure,
but of unfinished work.

Sometimes a single sentence rearranges your entire compass.
Her words did.

I carried her words with me
into every decision after.

Once the dust settled—
when the next yes came—
I went back to school.

I earned my master's degree in Management.

Not because I needed another title.
But because I wanted to build better systems—
not just survive the broken ones.

I didn't chase the degrees.
They chased me—
and somewhere along the way,
they found the version of me
I was becoming all along.

Degrees that Found Me Playlist

"Learning to Fly" – Tom Petty

Degrees that Found Me Reflection

What did you pursue before you knew why?

What moment looked like a detour but turned into direction?

Who said something that still echoes in your choices?

TRACK 7.5 COACH

The summer after my first year of college,
I coached girls' softball.
That was the last time.

There was so much complaining.

Didn't want to wear helmets—

might mess up the hair.
Wanted to play shortstop—
but were afraid of the ball.

I was nineteen.
And not quite built
for that kind of chaos in lip gloss.

So I moved on
to something way easier:
coaching three boys' baseball teams
at the same time.
T-ball.
Peewees.
Midgets.
All mine.

At the first coach's meeting,
They introduced me like a disclaimer.
There wasn't much applause.
It was more like mumbling,
side-eyes,
and a not-so-subtle wave of
"a girl coach?"

Then a kid named Eric—
Mature beyond his years—
stood up and offered this gem of encouragement:
"Be nice, guys—if she sucks, then we'll be mean."

Fair.

Turns out, I didn't suck.

I coached them for three years.
And we didn't just win.
We learned how to win.

We practiced hard
but had fun.
We ran laps to "Hakuna Matata."
We had trick plays from 2nd base to home.

We laughed. A lot.
But we also had rules.
A point system.
Because character counts more than batting averages.

+1 for good team communication on plays.
+2 for a double play.
+3 for displaying exemplary sportsmanship.

-1 for a strikeout.
-2 for an error.
-3 if you put someone down.

You strike out?
You still cheer the next kid on.
You miss the ball?
Your teammate shows up with support,
not sarcasm.

That was the culture.
That was the code.

After each game,
we checked the points.

If they were in the hole?
Laps. Pushups. Accountability.

One game they were in the positive.
Which meant Coach
had to do the push-ups.
At home plate.
While the boys counted.
And the parents cheered, and took pictures.

Not because I had to—
but because that's who I was.

That's what they remember.
More than the wins.
More than the stats.
The day their coach
followed the rules too.

Because you can't preach accountability
if you're not willing to drop and give 'em ten.

Those boys were special.
We only lost one game
in three years.

They weren't just good ball players.
They were good humans.
And they grew up to win
state championships
in basketball and football.

I'd like to think

some part of that started with
"Be nice—if she sucks, then we'll be mean."

That was the end of my coaching era—
for a while.
Until years later,
when I dusted off my whistle
and coached Nathan's 5th grade
school and YMCA basketball teams.

Still fun.
Still fierce.
Still full of heart.
Still no room
for putting people down.

I thought I was there to coach them.
But those boys taught me too.
About leadership.
About consistency.
About how respect is earned
in reps,
in laughs,
and in following through—
even when it means doing pushups
at home plate.

Turns out,
my first real team
wasn't in a boardroom,
a classroom,
or a coaching program.
It was a dugout.

Filled with dirt,
dreams,
and a group of kids
who gave me more than I ever gave them.

Coach Playlist

"Centerfield" – John Fogerty

Coach Reflection

Who was the first person or group that gave you a shot—even if they didn't realize it?

What "game" did you learn the most from, even if it wasn't the one you expected?

If someone watched how you lead others, what would they say your culture is?

TRACK 7.6 JOBS, JOY, AND JUST ENOUGH SLEEP

I didn't have a college job.
I had a collage of them.
And somehow, it worked.

Jet Photo:

I already knew my way around the chemicals—
thanks to a summer in high school behind the counter

at the Walmart photo lab.

But Jet Photo was faster.
Tighter.
More precise with everyone's 35mm memories.
The kind of place where you had to be quick
but careful—
especially when they handed over 110 film.

Those tiny negatives were delicate,
like threading memories through a sewing needle.

Sometimes people would
expose a little too much of themselves—
if you know what I mean.

We'd print a roll,
take one look,
and hand it off
without a word.

We didn't judge.
We just printed.
Let people keep their moments,
messy or magical.

Some rolls were birthday cakes
and football games.
Others were funerals and goodbyes.
Hospital visits,
vacations,
surprise tattoos,
and quiet things they maybe didn't mean to capture.

It taught me early
that people are complicated.
And sometimes,
the quiet work behind the counter
reveals more than what's developed.

I learned to treat every roll like it mattered.
Because sometimes
it really, really did.

Doc & Eddy's:

It wasn't a college bar.
But it was the kind of place
where half the staff
was trying to finish homework
between happy hour and the dinner rush.

A restaurant and bar combo—
sports on the TVs,
baskets of fries,
prime sandwiches we couldn't make fast enough,
and a shift schedule written in pencil
because someone was always swapping.

I was a server.
A bartender.
A pitcher-toting, dart-throwing,
table-running college kid
who hadn't quite learned
how to say no to extra shifts.

I worked with friends—

and sometimes we drove each other nuts—
but we laughed hard,
sang to the jukebox,
and made tips just big enough
to feel like freedom.

It had its moments of drama.
Late clock-ins.
Flirtations, fallouts,
kitchen meltdowns,
manager mood swings,
and at least one broken heart per double shift.

There were nights we'd close together,
clean the line while talking about future dreams,
and sneak fries before last call.

And then...
there was that night.
A packed Friday dinner rush.
My first ovarian cyst decided
to make its debut.

No warning.
Just a bolt of pain—
like something inside me tore open
while I was printing a ticket
for another damn prime sandwich.

I doubled over in the server station.
Held my breath through the spasms.
And still ran food to table six
because quitting

wasn't on the menu.

I didn't know what was happening—
but I knew how to keep going.

And that's what Doc & Eddy's gave me:
A crash course
in showing up anyway.

In holding pain and presence
in the same breath.

And in learning that sometimes,
the lesson behind the bar
has nothing to do with alcohol—
and everything to do
with becoming someone
who gets the job done,
no matter what's burning inside.

Boys' Baseball:

I coached three boys' baseball teams at the same time.
T-ball, peewees, and midgets.
Yes, all at once.
Yes, while doing everything else.
Yes, they doubted me.
No, they didn't win that bet.
But that deserves its own track—
and it got one.

The Safe House:

I worked the overnight shift.
$10 a night.
That's what they paid
to have someone stay
just in case.

Most nights were quiet.
A tired kind of quiet.
The kind that settles
after chaos has already happened.

It was a house for women escaping violence.
Women with bruises in places they didn't point to,
kids who held silence like armor,
and stories that walked in
without needing to be told.

I could sleep on the job.
But usually I stayed up.
Listened for footsteps.
Checked the doors.
Kept the lights low
and the TV softer.

It was one of the only jobs
where I felt calm.
Where just being there
was enough.
I usually felt safe—
even though I was young.
Even though I was often alone.

But once—

just once—
something felt off.
A knock that didn't sound right.
A shadow too close to the window.
My gut went cold
before my hand reached for the phone.

I called the police.
Backup came.
Nothing happened—
but everything could have.

That night taught me
that safety isn't just about locks.
It's about presence.
Awareness.
And the courage to act
before you're sure you need to.

One summer,
the Safe House got a donation—
a new stove and fridge.

They gave me the old ones.
That summer, I furnished my rental with secondhand
appliances
from a house built on survival.

It felt nice.
To be held up
by something that once held others.

Campus Jobs:

Mailroom.
Bookstore.
Admissions Office.
Football team tutor.
I worked them all—
the full campus trifecta,
plus a little academic triage on the side.

Work-study made it possible
to stay afloat
without adding more loans
to an already overloaded backpack.

In the mailroom,
I sorted envelopes
and delivered packages
to people who barely looked up.

It wasn't glamorous,
but there was something steady about it.
Alphabetical order.
No drama.
Just systems and silence.
A little peace
in a life that never stopped buzzing.

At the bookstore,
I rang up textbooks students couldn't afford,
and sold overpriced granola bars
to people running late to class.

But Admissions—
that's where it shifted.

I wasn't just clocking in.
I was leading campus tours,
organizing student ambassadors,
representing a college
that had become more than a school to me—
it was a lifeline.

I helped students say yes to their future,
even when I wasn't sure what mine would be.

I told stories about community,
about connection,
about finding your place—
while quietly learning how to hold my own.

I didn't know it then,
but those shifts would come in handy.

A few years later,
I'd step into a full-time role
as Assistant Director of Admissions
at another university.
Similar energy.
New office.
Different shoes.

And then there was the Study Table.
A room full of football players,
headphones half-on,
assignments half-finished,
trying to stay eligible
and awake.

I sat with them.
Walked them through math problems,
proofread papers,
and reminded them
what was due tomorrow.

Some were grateful.
Some rolled their eyes.
But I kept showing up.
Because behind every GPA
was someone holding it up.
And for a few hours each week,
that someone was me.

They were just jobs.
But also not.
They gave me structure.
Confidence.
A tiny slice of identity
on a campus that asked me to show up
again and again.

Summer Nanny:

For three summers,
I cared for two kids
who became like family.

They had a pool—
so add lifeguard
to the never-ending job list.
I kept watch
over cannonballs, snack times,

sunburns, sibling spats,
and one inflatable flamingo
that didn't make it past July.

Their mom would head out of town—
sometimes for a weekend,
sometimes for work—
and I'd step in.

School year or summer.
Homework help or bedtime stories.
I fed them.
Drove them.
Cleaned up after them.
Laughed with them.

They were loud,
opinionated,
endlessly curious—
just like me.
And they trusted me
with all of it.

Katelyn, the youngest,
once rode five hours with me
to visit my family's farm in North Dakota.

She made herself right at home—
boots in the doorway,
questions for my dad,
treats from the fridge like she belonged there.
Because she kind of did.

She even went out to check the cows,
her tiny frame climbing up the fence,
watching them lumber toward us
like she'd done it a hundred times.

We weren't just passing time.
We were building trust
one popsicle,
one pool day,
one pickup at a time.

They didn't pay enough to retire early.
But some jobs aren't about the money.
They're about showing up
in the background of someone's childhood
and knowing you made it a little bit softer

State Training School:
Intern. Emergency Staff.

They called me Ms. Morrison.
I was barely older than most of them,
but the title made it easier
to draw the line
between me
and where they were.

One of the boys told me
I looked like Sheryl Crow.
He was lying,
but I let him have it.
A little charm
goes a long way

when your days are measured in lockdowns and lineups.

They were there for different reasons.
A drive-by shooting.
Molesting younger children.
One boy told me,
quiet and direct:
"I never want to be released.
Because I know I'll do it again."
What do you say to that?
I said nothing.
I just sat there.
Present.
Still.
Heavy.

We played basketball
and checkers.
They showed me how to make scrambled eggs
with pepper
and brown sugar—
a combo
that somehow tasted amazing.

We laughed sometimes.
I smiled often—
but never completely.
I was always a little on edge,
waiting for someone to snap.

No one really ever did.
Not really.
We had to do restraints once.

He screamed and kicked,
but it wasn't violence
I could hear it in his voice—
It was grief.
Desperation.
A roar
from a boy who wanted
someone to hold his pain
without needing a reason.

It was the only job
where the rules and the humanity
collided so hard
I sometimes forgot which side I was on.
But I kept showing up.
With boundaries,
yes.
But also with belief
that even in a place built to contain,
connection could still slip through the cracks.

And now, years later—
I'm not the one in those halls anymore.
But my wife is.
She teaches inside the prison.
And at the youth correctional center.
She stands in rooms
I once walked through,
offering the same kind of presence—
firm, soft, steady.

And together,
we carry a legacy

of showing up
for those the world gave up on too soon.

Wrap Around Project:

Most of the kids were one signature away
from being sent somewhere they'd never come back from.

Behavioral issues,
they called it.
But sometimes it wasn't behavior—
just heartbreak
that had nowhere else to land.

I wasn't there to judge.
Or punish.
Or write referrals.
I was just there.
To listen.
To show up.
To be one adult
who wasn't put on this earth
to discipline them.

Sometimes we talked.
Sometimes we didn't.
Sometimes they'd pretend not to care
while secretly tracking every word.
They knew why I was there.
And more importantly—
they knew I came back.

Week after week.

Without fanfare.
Without promises.
Without trying to fix them.
Just a steady presence
in the middle of a system
that had already decided
who they were.

The truth is—
they didn't need another program.
They needed a witness.
Someone who saw
the scared kid
behind the sharp mouth.
The quiet potential
behind the threat of failure.
Someone to wrap around
without wrapping them up in labels.

And now, decades later—
I do the same thing.
In classrooms.
In coaching calls.
In businesses.
In quiet conversations
where someone still needs to be seen
without being sorted.
Same heart.
Clearer eyes.
Stronger legs to stand in the margins.

And somehow,
between all of that—

I got four degrees.
Played sports.
Made lifelong friends.
Dated.
Danced.
Lost sleep.
And found parts of myself
I didn't know I had.
Jobs, joy, and just enough sleep
to keep going.

Turns out, that collage of jobs
wasn't chaos—
it was a blueprint.
I didn't realize it then,
but I was building something
with every shift.

Not just a résumé.
Not just rent money.
But resilience.
Compassion.
Capacity.

I was learning how to read a room,
how to stay awake when others slept,
how to hear what wasn't being said,
and how to show up anyway.

Every job—
from checkers with incarcerated teens
to lunch rushes with impatient tables—
gave me a skill

I'd use later.
In boardrooms.
In coaching sessions.
In hospital rooms.
In motherhood.
In love.

And maybe that's the truth
no one tells you when you're twenty,
tired,
and juggling ten things at once:
The life you're building
while you think you're just getting by—
is the life you'll one day be grateful you survived.

Jobs, Joy, and Just Enough Sleep Playlist

"Something More" – Sugarland
"She Works Hard for the Money" – Donna Summer

Jobs, Joy, and Just Enough Sleep Reflection

Think back to a season of your life when you were holding more than anyone knew.

What did that version of you teach you about grit, presence, or capacity?

What jobs (paid or unpaid) shaped the way you love, lead, or listen today?

TRACK 7.7 DETOURS, DITCHES, AND DRESSES

In college,
I "dated" a guy named Troy Martini.
We met at a Human Services convention
in Indianapolis.
Talked about marriage
by day three.

He was older.
A bodybuilder.
A security guard
who had gone back to school.

The first time I drove to visit him in
Topeka, Kansas—
somewhere south of Omaha—
I got a flat tire.

As I pulled the jack from the trunk,
a man on a motorcycle pulled over.
"I've got this," I said.
He insisted.
He slapped on the baby tire,
then waved me to follow him.
We pulled into a little shop.
He talked to the owner,
then turned to me and said:
"They'll take care of you. It's already paid for."
I argued.
He just smiled.

"I have a good job.
Pay it forward someday."
Then rode off like some leather-clad angel,
on a random Thursday.

I don't remember much about my visits.
Troy worked a lot.
Lived in a sketchy part of town.
Had weights instead of furniture.
I'm not saying that's a red flag...
but when your couch is a bench press, maybe don't talk about
marriage on day three.

I think I watched Jeopardy
while he made grilled chicken
and told me I should try protein powder.

The second time I visited,
another highway incident.
North of Omaha,
a car stuck deep in mud in the median.
Didn't think much of it.

But then—
at the next gas stop—
a man approached me.
Looked and sounded exactly like Bobby McFerrin.

Thick accent.
Gentle smile.
"My cah is stuck.
Can you he'p me?"
I had a Grand Am.

Not exactly built for heroic rescues.
But I tried.
We even tried using our floor mats
for traction.
Mud everywhere.

Finally, a guy in a pickup
tow-roped him out of the ditch.
I was preparing to leave
when he stopped me.
"Wait," he said.
"You come wit' me.
To Wah-shin-ton Dee Cee.
We get maaa-rried.
I become U.S. *cit-uh-zin.*"

So...
that's when the pay-it-forward train
came to a screeching halt.
I peeled out,
mud and all.
Didn't even grab my floor mats.
Early wedding present to him and the future Mrs.

I never saw Troy again.
Didn't need to.
Even though
I had the bridesmaid dresses already picked out—
rainbow-colored
Southern Belle-type nightmares.

Funny thing is—
I don't actually remember the breakup.

There wasn't one.
No dramatic phone call.
No final letter.
Just the slow fade
of landlines and long-distance stamps.

We didn't have cell phones.
No internet.
No statuses to update.
Just silence
that eventually stayed quiet.

When I told my mom
we wouldn't be getting married,
she exhaled a prayer:
"Thank God.
I knew I couldn't tell you what to do.
So I just prayed
you'd make the right decision."

And somehow,
between flat tires,
muddy medians,
and marriage proposals at gas pumps,
I did.

Because growing up
doesn't always look like
stability or sense—
sometimes, it just looks like
turning the car around
before the rainbow dresses
ever make it out of the JCPenny catalog.

Years later,
he reached out again.
But I had already moved on—
with my own protein powder
and a better sense of direction.

Sometimes,
growth doesn't come with fanfare or final words.
It comes with a flat tire,
a stranger's kindness,
and the slow realization
that you've outgrown the story
before it ever really began.

Detours, Ditches, and Dresses Playlist

"Don't Worry, Be Happy" – Bobby McFerrin

Detours, Ditches, and Dresses Reflection

Who were the people or places you once imagined a future with—
and how did you know it was time to let go of the version of you that fit inside that life?

TRACK 7.8 A FRIEND'S A FRIEND FOREVER

I had so many
subsets of friends.

One group
still checks in via Snapchat—
our group name: DWU 44+
(which is adorable,
since all of us are now DWU 50+,
still sending memes, marking milestones,
and flat-out refusing to graduate from inside jokes).

This crew is solid.
The best.
The kind of friends who remember your dog's name
and your worst breakup.
The kind of women who show up—with snacks,
your favorite drink from 1997,
and blaring "I'm Gonna Be (500 Miles)"
like it's still the peak of our mixtape years.

All are teachers,
except Laurie—our outlier with a teaching degree
and a career in PT,
and me.
Though now, I guess I qualify too—
as a higher ed prof
teaching more than just curriculum.
Call it lived experience.
Call it office hours with soul.
Call it whatever you want—
but somehow,
I ended up at the front of the room too.

One year we took a road trip to Nebraska
to visit Tasha—
the married-with-kids one,

the one who made adulting look effortless
even when it probably wasn't.

That's when the traveling belt was born—
a ridiculous oversized plastic WWE championship belt
we used for the official contests of pure nonsense.

That night, the game was this:
Flirt with a stranger,
but not just any stranger—
you had to approach the exact person
you were assigned
the moment they walked through the door.

Mine was at least 110 years old.
Penny's walked out before she could make eye contact.
Robin invited hers over,
but struck out—
We gave her points for effort and flair.
D and Tasha were the married ones,
laying low,
taking in all the craziness
like anthropologists observing the wild.
Laurie?
She invited hers to our table.
He joined us.
She won.

For a while, that thing showed up
at birthdays,
baby showers,
and parties.

Then it just... disappeared.
Can't be found.
Secretly,
I think Laurie just never wanted to let it go.
And honestly?
I wouldn't have either.

Some of my other friends,
I still see.
Some I only heart and like on social media.
Some taught me how to laugh louder.
Some taught me to watch my back.

But Traci's been stitched into my life since the first college
chapter.

She is Dolly.
I am Lorrie (Morgan).
She is Kit.
I am Viv.

One summer, we wrote Pretty Woman 2
in full sincerity—
and to this day,
Vivian Ward is still my unofficial stage name.

We cried—hard—to Michael W. Smith's
A Friend's a Friend Forever,
as if it were scripture.
And in a way,
it was.

That one summer,

I went with her to a street dance
in Scotland.
(The tiny town in South Dakota—
not the country.).
That's where her grandma lived.

We got into a massive fight.
She wanted to stay out and keep the night going.

I wanted to go to bed.
She didn't want me walking back to her grandma's without her.
I didn't want to leave her alone, either,
especially since she thought she might be pregnant.

I don't remember what she said—
but I remember how I reacted.

I literally lifted her off the ground.
Like I was about to toss her
into another time zone.

Then I turned around
and started walking.

No cell phones back then.
No Uber.
No "share location"
or "drop a pin."

Just me, 53 miles from home,
in a rage,
at a bar
in the middle of nowhere.

It smelled like
deep-fried everything
and stories no one asked to live.

I stepped inside—
sweaty, stubborn,
still shaking from our fight.

"Can I use your phone?" I asked the bartender.
He pointed.
Didn't ask why.

I made a collect call
to a guy from my coed softball team.
He came.
Fifty-three miles
on a Saturday night
to pick up a girl
who was good at hitting triples
and burning bridges
at inconvenient times.

He dropped me off.
I exhaled.
And waited for
forgiveness
or fallout—
whichever came first.

A few days later,
I went to the pool where she was lifeguarding
to apologize.

She met me
with softness—
and the news
that she was going to have a baby.
The fight became just a story to laugh about in the future.

We lacked no imagination.
Or flair for the dramatic.

Like the night we
transformed Teresa, her twin sister's (also the cheerleader who
dug through my tape collection) apartment
into the most sacred of spaces—
a stage.

It was called The Hart Theater.
Not for the Broadway glow,
but because that was her last name.
And we had flair for the literal
and the dramatic.

I guess
you could have called it
dinner theater—
if dinner meant Chinese takeout
eaten cross-legged on the floor,
and wine that came in
cheap bottles
labeled Boone's Farm.

The stage was a living room.
The lighting:
a crooked lamp with a burnt-out bulb.

But the performances?
Tony-worthy.
In our minds, anyway.

We put on
a full-blown, impromptu acting night—
a self-curated class
where we each wrote scene prompts,
little emotional grenades
for the other to perform.

"You just found out you have cancer."
"You're a long-lost twin meeting your sister on a cruise ship."

Traci cried on cue.
I monologued in a borrowed robe.

The camera never blinked.

At some point, we swayed and sang along
to Strawberry Wine
like we were the last girls
standing at prom.

We weren't actresses.
We were alchemists—
turning a two-bedroom walk-up
into a memory
that still takes center stage
decades later.

We were in each other's first weddings.
We're still in each other's lives.

Her daughter—
who now has three beautiful kids of her own, and still calls me
Auntie Nik—
And that
feels exactly right.

Because some friendships
don't fade with time—
they stretch,
grow,
and multiply.

After all...
A friend's a friend forever—
even if, at one point,
you nearly launched them
into a cornfield
in Scotland, South Dakota.

A Friend's a Friend Forever Playlist

"Friends" – Michael W. Smith
"Strawberry Wine" – Deana Carter
"I'm Gonna Be (500 Miles)" – The Proclaimers

A Friend's a Friend Forever Reflection

Think of a friend who's known every version of you.
What scene do you remember most vividly with them?

What part of that memory makes you laugh?

What part still brings tears?

If you could thank them for one thing, what would it be?

Write a letter to that friend—even if you never send it.

TRACK 7.9 ALWAYS THE BRIDESMAID

I was never the queen.
Not in high school.
Not in college.
Not in love.

Homecoming court?
Yes.
Crown?
No.

Miss Wesleyan finalist?
Yes.
Winner?
No.

Then came the stages that didn't have dresses—
just podiums and spotlights.

2006
The National Business and Professional Women's Organization.
I'd won locally. Then state.
With a four-minute speech,
judges' interviews,

a stack of forms and fire in my voice.

At Nationals—
Runner-up, they said.

Lost by less than a point.

Almost harder than third—
because you can see first from there.

I didn't hear "#2 in the nation."
I heard "not #1."

I questioned everything,
wondering if it was that one question—
when they asked if I'd run
Republican or Democrat
if I ever ran for office—
and I said I wasn't sure.

My mentor Elyse believed in me.
Even more than I did.
I practiced my speech.
So many times at her dealership—
I swore I saw her sales guys
mouthing my lines while I practiced.
They probably could've delivered
the four minute speech themselves.

A few years later,
finalist again—
Outstanding Young North Dakotan.
Runner-up.

Always so close.
Always the bridesmaid.

Not just at the podium—
but in life.

I always made the short list,
but never the final cut.

When my friends started getting married,
I became a regular.
Bridesmaid dress on,
smile set,
heels swapped for sneakers
as soon as we hit the dance floor.

One time, I caught it.
Me.
I caught the bouquet.

And I didn't just hold it—
I ran a victory lap.
In tennis shoes under
my chiffon dress.

Everyone laughed.
So did I.

But deep down,
I wasn't laughing.

If I wasn't a bridesmaid,
I was probably the videographer.

That's what I get
for living with a camera on my shoulder for so many
years—
always recording other people's big moments,
rarely starring in my own.

Because I never really believed
I'd have my own wedding.

Not just because of timing.
Not just because of love.
But, because of who I wanted to love.

There was a sadness underneath the celebration.
A silent grief
every time someone else walked down the aisle
and I walked beside them
instead of toward someone waiting for me.

I smiled big, in all the photos.
Made great speeches.
Caught bouquets like they were destiny.
But I was always the bridesmaid.

And back then,
I truly believed
that's all I'd ever be.

Maybe being "runner-up"
was just the universe's way
of training me to stand beside people
until, I could finally stand beside
her.

Always the Bridesmaid Playlist

"You Can't Hurry Love" – The Supremes
"Dancing On My Own" – Robyn
"Part of Your World" – Jodi Benson

Always the Bridesmaid Reflection

When in your life did you feel "included but not chosen"?
What did that feel like?

Have you ever smiled through a celebration that secretly broke
your heart?

What roles do you often play for others that leave you feeling
unseen?

Track 8 Revolving Closet Doors

I remember the Ellen episode—
the one where she accidentally outs herself in the airport.

It was 1997.
And suddenly, it was possible.
To say it.
Out loud.

On television.
I watched it with wide eyes.
Heart racing.
Mouth still shut.

I wouldn't say it for two more years.
I swallowed it.
Stuffed it down behind smiles,
inside safe answers,
beneath what everyone else needed me to be.

But when I did—
oh, when I did—
I didn't whisper.
I didn't inch.
I didn't ask for permission.

I kicked the damn closet doors clean off,
heart pounding,
lungs on fire,
and stepped out
for her.

A whole other grown-ass adult older than me.

Not just years—lifetimes.

She had lived a whole life
before I'd even turned legal.
Wiser.
Sharper.
Weathered.
And exactly the kind of wild
my truth had been waiting for.

And I,
at twenty-six,
with barely a map of myself,
ran straight into her storm
like it was the only home I'd ever known.

She was out,
open,
loud,

funny,
surrounded by people who lit up in her orbit.
I needed to meet her.
I needed to tell her.
So I did.

I found her address in the phone book—
yes, the actual printed kind—
and showed up at her door.
To profess my love.
To console her (her mom had just passed)
To say,
"I see you. And I love you."

She patted me on the head,
like I was a well-meaning love-drunk puppy,
and said,
"We'll talk about this another time."

We dated.
Lived together.
On again, off again.
But I was smitten.
She was my first gay love.

My mom was staying with me that winter.
She did that during the holidays—
working at the post office through the busy Christmas holiday
mail rush.

She left early that year.
Said she couldn't handle the news.
Said Dad couldn't either.

They didn't talk to me for months.

Eventually they came around—
a little.
As long as we didn't talk about it.
As long as I lived a quiet kind of love.
Don't Ask, Don't Tell
wasn't just military policy.

I never liked labels.
Not for my sexuality,
not for my politics,
not for my faith.
I'm just me.
Why does everyone want us boxed,
tagged,
shelved?

I had crushes on three of my friends growing up.
Grade school through college.
I think one or two probably knew.
I'll let them guess and duke that out.
Not spilling that in this book.

After we broke up,
We still lived together.
I didn't do well.
I lived on hope—
and nothing else.

I had this little book called *Hope to Hang On To*.
Filled with quotes.
I dated each one as I read it,

so I wouldn't accidentally repeat the same hope twice.

Mantras.
Whispers.
Lifelines.

I journaled.
About feeling lost.
About not knowing if I'd ever find true love.
Or freedom.
Or anything more than survival.

Because the truth is—
coming out of the closet
was the biggest move I had ever made
for myself.

Not a job.
Not a degree.
Not even a move across state lines
compared to the weight of saying:
This is who I love.
This is who I am.

It felt bold.
And terrifying.
And permanent.
And when it ended,
I didn't just feel heartbroken—
I felt exposed.
Unloved and unfinished.

I played MASH.

Yes, the game.
Trying to trick fate into telling me who my soulmate was.
"Unknown" was always one of the options.

After two years out of the closet,
I went back in.
Hard.

Greg helped me move out.
Made cookies
and left them outside my door before work in the mornings.
That's where his chapter begins.
And where Disc Three begins as well.

Revolving Closet Doors Playlist

"Pink Pony Club" – Chappell Roan
"Both Sides Now" – Joni Mitchell
"Foolish Games" – Jewel
"Iris" – The Goo Goo Dolls

Revolving Closet Doors Reflection

What was the first truth you ever whispered to yourself—
but were afraid to say out loud?

Have you ever fallen in love with someone before you were
ready to be seen?

In what ways have you tried to "go back in" after stepping into
your truth?

What gave you hope when you couldn't find answers?
A quote?
A song?
A friend?
A tiny moment that kept you breathing?

What closet are you still circling?

What version of you is waiting to be welcomed home?

Track 9 End of Disc Two – Break the Silence

Not every silence is broken
by a shout.

Some are cracked open
by a whisper.
A sideways glance.
A confession made
to the wrong person
at the right time.

This disc held
the almosts.

The sashes and titles,
the bouquets caught and then clutched
like proof that someone, somewhere,
once saw me.

It held the crushes I never named,
the love I chased
before I knew how to love myself,
and the moments I disappeared
just to keep the peace.

I came out.
Then went back in.
I let myself be chosen—
and then abandoned pieces of myself trying to stay.

I stayed quiet in rooms
where I wanted to be loud.
And laughed loudly in rooms
where I still didn't feel seen.

But make no mistake—
something in me shifted here.
In the heartbreak.
In the hesitation.
In the hope I hung onto
even when I didn't believe it.

That little book of quotes,
those MASH scribbles,
the feeling of being
brave for five minutes
and paying for it for years—
it all belonged here.

If Disc One was hiding,
and Disc Two was learning how to say hard things,

then Disc Three?
Disc Three is the mic drop.
The revival.
The remix.
And baby—
it's going to be loud.

DISC THREE:
Full Volume

DISC THREE: Full Volume

They say healing whispers.
But mine?
It roared.

It didn't arrive in stillness,
soft hands,
and sage-scented surrender.

It came
after the breaking.
After the hiding.
After the nearly didn't-make-it.

This part of the story
doesn't tiptoe.
It kicks the damn door open.

Because survival is quiet.
But coming back to life?

That shakes the walls.

This part
is about turning up the dial
on everything I muted
just to stay likable,
safe,
digestible.

This part
is about saying the thing
I was never supposed to say—
not out loud.
Not without apology.

It's the volume
my truth was always meant to be played at.

It's the song
I hummed under my breath
for decades
while everyone danced
to something I didn't believe in.

This is where I stop
asking for understanding
and start standing
in the understanding I've earned.

I used to think
wholeness meant being quiet.
Polished.
Unbothered.

Forgiving without ever being fully heard.

But healing?
Real healing?
It doesn't come dressed in perfection.
It's raw.
It's ugly crying.
It's shaking hands writing hard truths
into the pages you promised
you'd never open again.

This part of the book
isn't about anyone else's comfort.
It's about mine.

It's about volume.
Full volume.
The kind that doesn't flinch
when someone walks in.
The kind that doesn't hit mute
just because someone you love
might not like the lyrics.

I won't lower it anymore.
This is where
the girl who made herself small
to keep others okay
finally takes up space.

Not to be loud.
But to be whole.

So if you're still reading—

if you're still with me—
turn the page.
Turn the dial.

It's time to rock!

Disc Three Full Volume Playlist

"Me" – Kelly Clarkson
"Don't Let the Light Go Out" – Panic! At The Disco

Disc Three Full Volume Reflection

Where in your life are you still hitting mute?

What parts of your story do you whisper, when they deserve to be shouted—or at least spoken?

Whose comfort are you still protecting at the expense of your own truth?

What would "full volume" look and feel like for you—emotionally, creatively, relationally?

Finish this sentence:
If I were living at full volume, I would...

Then do one small thing today that turns your dial even a notch higher.

Track 10 Lifetime Movie (Uncensored Version)

I've lived through things
that would sound like fiction—
the kind of scenes you watch
through cracks of your fingers
during a Lifetime movie night.

There were moments
when I thought I'd die on a sidewalk.
Not metaphorically.
Not in a "this breakup is killing me" kind of way.

But literally—
that she might drive up onto the curb
and take me out
just because I existed.

Because I was going to marry the man
she used to control.
Because I became stepmother

to the children
she used as weapons.
Because I fell for someone
she still wanted the power to destroy.

She keyed my car
and poured oil across the windshield
outside my workplace.
Wrote "Lesbian gone bi"
in scratches across the paint
on my prized Subaru.

She keyed our ladder.
Our grill.
She trespassed into our backyard
like it was her war zone.
She wasn't even fighting a war.
Just haunting one she already lost.

The night before our wedding,
she dropped off
love letters she and he had written when they were young.
She was already remarried.
The cruelty wasn't confusion.
It was calculated.

She called the school
pretending to be me—
demanding to be billed
for tuition she never paid.

She called me pretending
to be a hospital

collecting on her son's ski injury.
She was an evil shapeshifter.
A voicemail villain.
A master of manipulation
with just enough crazy
to be dangerous
and just enough cunning
to be believable.

She attacked me
while I was pregnant.
I had to get a restraining order
while pregnant with the child
who now flinches
when his heart races too fast.
Anxiety.
It lives in his bones like it once lived in mine.

I had my first ever panic attack
holding a microphone,
about to ask Ann Whitman,
the CEO of eBay,
a question
at a leadership conference.
I stood up,
and it felt like a surge of static—
like a live wire between
my chest and brain—
short-circuited.

I almost blacked out.
I didn't even know
what was happening.

It wasn't fear of the stage.
It was trauma.
It was unprocessed.
It was lodged in my nervous system
like an unpaid bill
she kept sending to my body.

I went to more doctor visits.
My blood pressure rose.
And no one on the outside
would've guessed
I was being hunted
by someone who thought
She was the victim.

For nine years,
she badmouthed us
to anyone who would listen—
and to the ones who wouldn't,
She tried harder.

And still—
I showed up.
For the kids.
For him.
For our future.
For my own dignity.
Because she wasn't going
to be the reason
I forgot how to live.

I don't write this
to vilify her.

I write this
because my body
has held the silence long enough.

And because I will not
let this story
be edited out
just because it's inconvenient.

This isn't drama.
It's documentation.
This is the movie
no one would believe
if I hadn't lived it.

What I Would Say to Her Now:

I don't hate you.
That would take too much energy.
And I've learned to spend mine wisely.

I used to want an apology.
Now I want nothing from you.
Not even understanding.
Because healing means
you don't get to live rent-free in my mind anymore.

You don't get to shake my body
like an earthquake no one else sees.

You were chaos
dressed in entitlement
masquerading as motherhood.

You weaponized love
because you didn't know how to hold it.
And I was never your target.
Just the nearest reflection
of what you hadn't yet faced.

But here's what you didn't count on:

I kept records.
Literal ones.
Cassette tapes.
Of you pretending to be a hospital bill collector—
and then slipping out of character mid-call.

I've never replayed them.
Never needed to.
Because the truth doesn't get louder with volume.
It just waits,
quiet and certain,
like evidence that doesn't require a courtroom.

But what I did do—
I helped him stay grounded.
When rage knocked,
we answered with restraint.
When chaos baited,
we took the higher road.

Every time.

And that road—
the one paved with patience,
boundaries,

and so many quiet sacrifices—
led somewhere.

It didn't always feel fair.
But now, years later, I see the return:
Respect. Relationship.
The kind of love you only get by showing up for the hard parts
with integrity.

You gave him a blueprint for bitterness.
We built something better.
Because I refused to teach your children
that revenge was love in disguise.

So I'll say this once—
not for you,
but for me:

I faced it.
I faced you.
And I faced myself.

And I chose to become someone
you couldn't hurt anymore.

I wish you peace.
Because hurting people
hurt people.

And I am
done
hurting.

———

The tapes are still there.
Still waiting.
But I never pressed play.
Because I didn't need to hear her twice.

I walked away from that storm
with pieces of me still intact—
but not untouched.

You can't dodge nine years of madness
without flinching at shadows.
Without learning
what silence costs.
Without wondering
what you did
to make someone
hate you that much
for simply being alive
and loved.

But I didn't break.
I bent,
I wept,
I recorded the voicemails
and the evidence
and the doubts.

Then I looked in the mirror
to meet the parts
she didn't touch—
but I still hadn't made peace with.

This is where I stop surviving her.
And started becoming me.

Lifetime Movie Playlist

"Fighter" – Christina Aguilera
"Elastic Heart" – Sia

Lifetime Movie Reflection

Have you ever stayed silent for the sake of peace, only to realize it was costing you your own?

What "cassette tapes" from your life—literal or metaphorical—are you still holding onto them?
Do you need to press play...
or finally let them go?

Who did you help stay grounded, even while you were breaking?

What's one moment in your life where you took the high road when you could've burned it all down?

Track 11 Coming Out...
Again (Because Once
Apparently Wasn't Enough)

I used to think
you only came out once.
Like a dramatic exit
from behind the velvet curtain.

Cue the applause.
Cue the acceptance.
Cue the identity.

But turns out—
it's more like peeling paint.

You come out again,
and again—
each time stripping back
a version of yourself
you wore to survive.

Some layers come off clean.
Some cling like skin.
And underneath?
Just you.
Still standing.
Still trying to match
the inside to the outside.

Am I gay?
Bi?
Lesbian?
Fluid?

Still not sure what fits.
Maybe just me.

I know I love a woman.
I know I love truth.
And I know that love
was never the problem.
Hiding was.

A boxless being in a world full of checkboxes?
Does it matter?
Do I need a label
just to feel seen?
Just to justify love?

Coming out once
was terrifying.
Coming out twice—
after a marriage,

after kids,
after years of playing "normal"—
was something else entirely.

This wasn't
high school drama
or college confusion.

This was
real-life
rip-it-all-open
Reshape-everything-you-thought-was-stable
change the course of your family
forever.

By the time I said it out loud,
I was already gone—
from the version of myself
that could keep pretending.
Gone from the easy answer.
Gone from the life that made sense
to everyone else.

Soon after I'd start to fall
for a woman
ten years younger than me—
who lived 22 hours away.
Try explaining that
at parent-teacher conferences.

I had Greg's blessing.
He didn't yell.
Didn't beg.

Didn't punish.
He let me go.

But that didn't make it easy.
It made it harder.
Because now
I didn't even have a villain.
Just my own truth
and the wreckage it would cause.

People love a story
with clear roles.
Villain. Victim. Hero.
It helps them sleep at night.

But what do you do
when the ex-husband is kind,
the new partner is gentle,
and you are the one
setting fire
to the house
you built together?

I don't mean metaphorically.
We laid the floors.
Hung the drywall.
Chose every cabinet,
every light fixture,
every damn paint swatch
like it meant something.

And it did.
But meaning

doesn't always equal staying.
Sometimes the house you build
can't hold the truth
you finally let in.

I didn't get to tell the boys.
Didn't get to sit them down,
to stumble through it
with love and fear
and too many metaphors.

Greg told them.
Told my parents, too.
He thought he was protecting me.
Thought they'd take it better from him.
But it wasn't his story to tell.

He thought he was shielding me
from their disappointment.
But it wasn't disappointment
that hit hardest.

My parents didn't rage.
Didn't yell.
They just stopped speaking.

Silence,
their signature move.
Like if they didn't say the words,
they wouldn't be true.

Nearly two years of
invisible holidays

and pretending I was just busy.

And the boys—
They were kids.
Kind. Curious.
Caught in the middle
of a story they didn't ask to be in.

I never got to explain it
the way I wanted to.
Never got to say:
This doesn't change my love for you.
This doesn't make me someone else.
This just makes me
more me.

There's a loneliness
in doing the right thing
when it looks so wrong
from the outside.

There's a grief
in watching people mourn you
when you're not even dead—
just finally alive.

This wasn't
a brave declaration.
This was
a quiet detonation.

A long, slow walk
into the kind of freedom

that doesn't throw parades—
just closes doors behind you
and dares you
to keep walking.

Coming out the second time
wasn't about revelation—
it was about reclamation.
About not letting someone else
summarize
my soul
on my behalf.

It was messy.
Uneven.
Unapologetically mine.

And even now,
I'm still coming out.
Not just to others—
but to myself.

Every day I choose
to live unhidden
is another version
of coming out
and staying out.

Coming Out... Again Playlist

"She Used to Be Mine" – Sara Bareilles
"Let it Go" – Idena Menzel

"I'm Coming Out" – Diana Ross

Coming Out... Again Reflection

Have you ever chosen something true—
even though it made you the "villain" in someone else's story?

What roles have you been cast in that never fit?

What truths are you still learning how to live out loud?

Track 12 Letting Me Go

Seven years into our marriage,
Greg let me go.

Not because he didn't love me—
but because he did.
He saw something missing in my eyes:
a flicker gone dim,
a hunger he knew he couldn't fill.

And instead of holding tighter,
he loosened his grip
and gave me room to breathe.

He didn't set me free out of anger.
He gave me back to myself
out of grace.
Out of gut-wrenching,
grown-up,
unselfish love.

More grace than I gave myself.

I didn't need permission—
but he offered it anyway.
Like a man handing you the key
to a door you were already halfway through.

And I walked through.
Not right away.
But eventually.
Into something new
that began
with a contract.

Not a love letter.
Not a kiss.
A promise.

Nic & Nik's Contract to Take Care of Themselves
(Yes, we named it that. Yes, it was adorable. Yes, it saved us.)

Physically
– Sleep at least 6 hours a night
– Work out 4 days a week
– Eat smart

Emotionally
– Have hobbies
– Read and stay sharp
– Journal
– Say "no" when it means "no"
– 30 minutes daily for yourself
– Monthly pampering

– No one gets to tell you what you can't do
– Be a glass ¾ full, not just ½
– Laugh daily
– Choose supportive friends
– Simplify. Stay present. Avoid autopilot.
– Pay yourself first
– Don't compare

It began as care.
It grew into friendship.
Then long nights of connection.
Eventually it became love.

Real. Messy. Expansive. Healing. Love.
A love that honored my body,
my clarity,
my expansion.

It evolved
into short trips to Arizona.
Eventually we couldn't stand to be apart,
and I made the move South.

I tried to make it work long-distance.
Greg and the boys were supposed to join me in Arizona.
I even found him a job.

But when he said no—
I said yes to trying anyway.
I sold magazines.
Then cars.
Then landed at a prep school
that treated me like gold

and let me work remotely
when the ache for my boys
punched through my ribcage.

I missed them.
Every day.
And every day, I carried a quiet weight
in my chest—
a deep, aching guilt
that whispered:
"You're bad for leaving."

But eventually
as you'll soon read
the ache broke through the dam.

But it wasn't just about Arizona.
The weight had roots
in a pew I once sat in.
In a church
that taught me that my truth could send me to hell.

So when I first began to realize I loved differently,
that I was different,
I tucked it away.

I learned that silence was safe.
That visibility was dangerous.
That my truth made me bad.

Years later,
Arizona brought that same pain back to the surface.
Different setting.

Same wound.
And guilt rushed the wound like salt,
disguised as motherhood.

But guilt isn't always truth.
Sometimes, it's just old programming
dressed up as protection.

And when I finally stopped running from it,
when I met that pain in my chest
and asked it what it needed,
it said:
"Love me like the church never did."
So I did.

And that's when I saw it clearly:
Arizona wasn't abandonment.
It was alignment.
It was me, choosing truth.

For the first time, out loud.
And modeling that—
to sons who would grow into men
who love honestly,
parent with compassion,
and hold space for truth—
wasn't a failure.

It was the greatest parenting gift I could have given.
Not because I was perfect.
But because I was present—
in my truth,
my values,

my self-love.

Greg and I?
We didn't fall apart.
We shifted.
We co-parented like teammates.
We showed our kids that love doesn't always mean staying
together—
sometimes it just means staying honest.

And the guilt?
It still knocks sometimes.
But now I answer the door with compassion,
and a whisper to my younger self:
"I got you. It's safe to speak our truth now."

Because here's the truth,
the real one:
Choosing yourself
isn't selfish.
It's sacred.
And it echoes through generations.

My sons saw it.
Not in speeches—
but in steps.
In the way I left,
and in the way I never stopped showing up.

Greg saw it.
Not in anger—
but in honor.
In the way we rewrote our love

into friendship
that never wavered.

And I?
I saw myself.
Not in the mirror—
but in the mirror of who I became
when I stopped shrinking
for anyone.

This isn't the story
of a family broken.
It's the story
of a woman reclaimed.

That's parenting—
not by the book,
but by truth & love.

Letting Me Go Playlist

"Let It Go" – James Bay
"Goodbye to You" – Michelle Branch
"Let It All Go" – Birdy & RHODES

Letting Me Go Reflection

Have you ever held onto something—or someone—because you
thought you should, even when your soul knew otherwise?

What beliefs about truth, worth, or parenting were handed to
you that no longer serve you?

If you gave yourself permission to choose alignment over approval, what door would you finally walk through?

Write a letter to the version of you who stayed too long, left too soon, or did the hard thing anyway. Remind them:
"You didn't fail. You told the truth."

Track 13 Two Nicoles, One Forever

We started out as friends.
Accountability partners.
Two women daring each other
to take better care of ourselves.
To show up for our own bodies
the way we'd always shown up
for everyone else.

It shifted
on a visit to see her in Arizona.
Something in the desert heat,
or maybe the way she looked at me,
turned the ground under my feet
into a new kind of solid.

Moving to Phoenix
was like rising again.
Like the sun there had been waiting
just for me—

to burn away what I had outgrown
and warm the parts of me
I thought would stay cold forever.

We were on again, off again—
until we weren't.

She needed to be sure
she was ready for a marriage
that came with two children.
I needed to be sure
She was ready to stay.

We've been engaged twice.
Married twice.
Each time a stronger yes—
leading us to forever.

She proposed first—
on a paddle board trip at Lake Powell.
I didn't know it was an engagement trip,
so I invited my friend Stephanie along.
Stephanie became our photographer that day,
catching the moment I tipped my hat,
said "yep,"
and the world shifted beneath us.

Almost a year later,
I proposed to her
at our favorite place—
a wide-open field
overlooking the train bridge.
The kind of place

where time slows down
and you can see
both where you've been
and where you're going.

Our first wedding was just for us.
Just our friend/officiant, Erin,
and our sisters—
in case anyone tried to object
at the second one.

A couple of months later
we married again,
this time in front of friends and family
with a celebration big enough
to match the miles we'd walked to get there.

I read her my vows—
stitched together
from pieces of the love songs
that had carried us here:

"Today and always,
I cross my very human, occasionally anxious heart
and promise to give all I've got
to make all your visions come true.

There's nothing I wouldn't do,
no end of the earth I wouldn't walk to,
to help you never question my love.
Baby, I'm going to choose you,
forever and ever, amen.

Our love is stronger, deeper,
and more powerful than any love song out there.

And I want you to know—
sometimes I will fail.
Sometimes I will let you down.
But many times,
I will knock it out of the park.

Because all of me,
loves all of you,
for all of our days."

She read me her vows—
her own words,
crafted from her heart.
Different, but the same
in what they promised.
A forever we were both
finally ready to claim.

And then, as if the vows
had opened the air around us,
our song began—
Better Place by Rachel Platten.
It's not the kind of song
that drowns you in strings and grandeur.
It's simple.
Honest.
The way love feels
when it's in the right hands.

Every word was us—

a reminder that the world
really does feel kinder,
brighter,
and more possible
when we're in it together.

People call us
My Nicole, Your Nicole.
Nicole 1, Nicole 2.
Nicole squared.
The Nicoles.
A lady at a food truck
once called us
Nicole and Spicy Nicole
because she needed a name
to yell when our order was ready—
and my Nicole orders her food at heat level 4 spicy,
while I'm more of a level -4.

Our same name
is usually only an issue
with medical stuff.
They always want to change my last name
and my birthdate.
Honestly, I'd love to be ten years younger.

We are equal parts
soft and steel,
level 4 and level -4,
then and now.

She is my safe place—
the one I can fall apart with

and still feel whole.
The one who can quiet my storms
without dimming my fire.

She is the steady to my sprint,
the pause to my push,
the laughter that breaks through my overthinking.

She knows my edges
and doesn't flinch.
Knows my shadows
and still leans in.

She is my mirror and my anchor,
my risk and my refuge.
She is the proof
that love can be both
wild and steady,
tender and unshakable—
the yin to my yang,
and the place I want to land
at the end of every day.

And if "Better Place" is our wedding song,
then "Issues" by Julia Michaels
is the one we laugh about being
our "other" song.

Because we've got them—
I've got mine,
she's got hers—
and somehow,
we trade them in for grace,

for second chances,
for the kind of love
that can carry both the pretty and the messy
without dropping either.

One night,
We went out to eat.

Between the quiet and the clinking of glasses,
she looked at me and said,
"Do you even like me anymore?"

The question sat between us—
gentle, but heavy.

We had brought our gratitude journals—
the ones I designed myself:
How do I love thee? Let Me Write the Ways.

365 days of noticing,
365 days of remembering.

I hadn't written in mine for days.
And when I did,
it was surface-level things—
thank you for helping me wash the dishes.

What happened to us?

How can I love someone more than air,
and still forget to breathe her in?

That night reminded me—

forever isn't a feeling.
It's a practice.
It's writing it down
and showing up
even when the pages feel blank.

We are proof
that love doesn't have to come easy
to be right.
That sometimes
you walk away to be sure—
and come back
because you know.

And in the quiet between all of that—
the paddle boards and train bridges,
the level 4 spice and the level -4 calm,
the name mix-ups and double introductions—
is the simple truth:
I am exactly where I once prayed to be.

And here's the part I will never forget:
I once came out,
went back in,
and came out again.
I spent years
wondering if I'd ever have the kind of love
I could stand in without flinching.
Now here I am—
married to a woman
with my same name,
the same last nerve sometimes,
and the same vision for the life we want.

Since I started writing this book,
she's completed three-fifths
of her Doctorate in Occupational Therapy degree.
I've stepped into a new role
as a business professor,
launched The FoundHers Table,
watched our youngest son turn twenty-one,
our oldest graduate college,
and helped raise a two-year-old.

Together, we've also begun shaping The Prism Project—
a space for resilience, truth, and belonging.
It's not about fixing LGBTQ+ people.
It's about helping everyone else
unlearn the stories
that ever made belonging conditional.

We don't have it all figured out yet,
but we know this:
when light passes through a prism,
it doesn't break—
it reveals every color
that was already there.

In many ways,
I hope this book is part of that light—
a mirror,
a crack,
a beginning.
A story that helps the world see
what love really looks like
when it's allowed to belong.

Nothing we have done
has been easy.
But we are built for hard.
We are built for us.

Two Nicoles.
One forever.
No objections.

If there's anything our story proves,
it's that sometimes you don't just find the love of your life—
you build it,
piece by imperfect piece,
until it can hold
the weight of forever.

And for me,
forever isn't just built from the big vows
or the milestones—
it's built from knowing
that no matter how the day unfolds,
I have a place to land,
a hand that reaches for mine,
and a heart that will always
make me feel like home.

Two Nicoles, One Forever Playlist

"To Make You Feel My Love" – Adele
"I Cross My Heart" – George Strait
"Better Place" – Rachel Platten
"Issues" – Julia Michaels

Two Nicoles, One Forever Reflection

Love stories aren't always fairy tales.
Sometimes they're road maps—
with detours, roundabouts,
and places you circle back to
because you realize they're where you belong.

This chapter isn't just about finding love—
it's about returning to it,
choosing it again and again,
even when the road isn't smooth.
It's the proof that the right person
doesn't just make life easier—
they make life truer.

Think about the love you've built.
Not the glossy moments,
but the ones held together by shared grit and stubborn hope.

What has your love survived?

What have you survived together?

And what will you keep building—
piece by imperfect piece—
so it can hold the weight of forever?

Track 14 My Flaws

I can list all my flaws.

Not with shame—
with precision.
With the kind of familiarity
that comes from carrying them
like skin.

Let's begin.

Severely cystic breasts.
3.62 pounds removed—
but not forgotten.

Ninety percent cysts.
Ten percent shame.
Zero regrets.

The scars wrap around me
like parentheses,
reminding me daily
of what I hated
and what I inherited.

They speak louder
than any compliment ever did.
They don't whisper.
They don't fade.
They frame the part of me
I used to hate—
and now,
the part I'm finally learning
to forgive.

It wasn't cosmetic.
It was survival.
It was a goodbye letter
to the pain
I didn't owe anyone
an explanation for.

Adios, tatas.
You were heavy in more ways than one.

A skin growth on my left leg
that bleeds when I shave.
Like it's punishing me
for trying to smooth things over.
Not dangerous.
Just inconvenient.
Like most things I've lived with.

Moles,
cut out and tested.
Benign threats
that taught me
how to worry before anything even happened.
Little dots of fear
that marked me for years.
Still do.

My weight—
my least-kept secret.
The world's favorite flaw to talk about
when they run out of things to say.

But I always had two go-to jokes about that:

No one would ever try to abduct me.

If I ever got sick, I had enough mass to outlast a famine.
It was never really a joke.
It was biology.
It was survival.
It was the kind of armor
I didn't ask for
but was grateful for
on my worst days.
They say the body creates fat
to protect you.
A fortress.
The body's last line of defense
against when the world won't stop throwing stuff at you.

I believe it.

I just don't want the protection anymore.
I want peace.
I'm ready for it to stop now.

Sometimes I stare
at the flaws in the things I own
the way I stare at myself.
My car—
door dings, cracked windshield.
Not my fault,
but mine to live with.

My house,
with its buckled floorboards
and cupboard doors missing
from a project that stalled out
years ago.

Sometimes I am my house.
Held together by plans
I forgot how to finish.

And then—
there's my fuse.
Short.
Sharp.
Occasional, but memorable.

A flash of heat
that burns through my words
before I can cool them.

My impatience?
Legendary.
Ask anyone I've lived with.
Ask my kids—
all three of whom came early.

Maybe they just knew
I wasn't built for waiting.
Maybe they weren't either.
We're a family of urgent arrivals
and lessons in slowing down.

I've always been a counter.
Even at fifteen,
I wasn't just writing in my journals—
I was tallying the words.
As if the number somehow made them
more real,
more worth keeping.

By twenty-five,
I could tell you exactly
how much money I'd made
every single day
of my adult life.

I don't know if it was discipline,
obsession,
or just my way
of keeping the intangible
pinned to the page.

Maybe I was just making sure
nothing slipped through the cracks.
Or maybe
I didn't trust my life
to be enough
without proof.

And here's one
I don't always admit:

I don't speak up—
not when it comes to feelings.
Not when the words are tender
and the risk is real.

Sometimes I keep things in
because it feels safer
to swallow my needs
than to say them out loud
and watch them fall flat.

I stay quiet
when I should ask.
I nod
when I want to cry.
I hold it all in
like it's my job
to be the steady one.
The unbothered one.
The strong one.

It's the kind of flaw

that looks like control
but is really just fear
wearing a well-practiced mask.

I've spent years
protecting everyone else
from the fullness of my heart.
Even now—
some of my truest feelings
are tucked in the corners
of poems
no one's read yet.

We all have scars
from half-finished fixes.

But don't get it twisted.
I'm not ashamed.
I'm honest.

Because here's one thing
you won't find
on any of my lists—
one thing I've never lost
to imperfection:

Integrity.

That one's not cracked.
It's not up for debate.
It's my whole damn foundation.

I say what I do.
I do what I say.

Even when I'm scared.
Even when I'm exhausted.
Even when I'm bleeding
from places that shouldn't bleed.

Even when I'm counting—
words,
dollars,
days survived—
not because numbers define me,
but because I need to know
I showed up for every single one.

It's my proof.
My receipts.
The ground I stand on.

That has never wavered.

And maybe that's why
I can stand here now
with a body that's been
bruised, cut,
stretched, stitched,
ignored, fed, feared,
and fiercely held together—
and say,
"This is me."

Flawed.

But never fake.

These flaws
aren't failures.
They're just part
of the architecture."

And I am
still standing.
Still learning.
Still here.

Full volume.

I thought my mind was the battlefield.
Then my body reminded me—
it had been at war, too.

My Flaws Playlist

"This is Me" – Keala Settle
"I'm Beautiful" – Bette Midler

My Flaws Reflection

We all carry lists—
of what we've been told is wrong with us,
of what we've believed without question,
of what we hide and what we use as armor.

What's on your unspoken list?

Which "flaws" have shaped your strength?

Where have you been protecting yourself in ways that no longer serve you?

Write your own list of flaws—but this time, write it with love.

What are you ready to forgive?

What are you finally ready to say out loud?

Track 15 The Body Remembers—and So Do You

Funny thing—
this was one of the last tracks I added.
Which is wild,
considering it's controlled my life
for 28 years.
You'd think it would've made the list sooner.

It started with a cyst—
a sudden rupture that sent me down a path
I never expected.

Endometriosis.
A word people whispered at the time,
or didn't know at all.
A condition doctors dismissed
or didn't understand.
Fibroids the size of golf balls and grapefruits.
Enormous pain.

And as if my uterus wasn't loud enough,
life added its own version:
A child protection client
threatened to kill me
because I was part of the team holding him accountable
for years of severe domestic and child abuse.
My sister's boyfriend
was killed in a motorcycle crash.
My grandfather passed away.

I had said I'd never move back to North Dakota.
Then I handed in my one-month notice,
packed my bags,
and left—job or no job.
It didn't matter—
I was moving back.
I did find a job just before I moved.
Higher education welcomed me in.

At 24, I was told I'd probably never have kids.
Recommended treatment?
A hysterectomy.
I got a new doctor.
After a laparoscopy,
she suggested Lupron Depot—
a medical menopause.
Spoiler alert:
Hell.

Hot flashes that felt like
I was on fire from the inside out.
Message boards said
even spouses wanted to jump off bridges.

No lies detected.

Then a nurse practitioner found
my thyroid was basically asleep.
Add that to the list.
And yet—
Nickolas came to be.

One or two tries.
It was February.
Greg and I were getting married in September.
I wanted to wait,
but he said,
"What if this is the only window?"
So we opened it.

After Nick was born,
I bled every single day
for seven months.
An endometrial ablation followed.
Doctors said:
"If you want another... start soon."
Another window, flung open.
Nathan arrived 11 months later.

Some people find relief through pregnancy.
I wasn't some people.

In 2006,
I had a hysterectomy—
the so-called cure.
It wasn't.
In 2010, another laparoscopy.

Then nearly a decade
on birth control to manage symptoms.
It helped...
until it didn't.

And yes—
I was on birth control
with no fishbowl (aka uterus),
and in a same-sex marriage.

Still had to prove to insurance
that it was "medically necessary."
Because apparently,
unless there's a chance of surprise conception,
pain doesn't count.

Forget the inflammation,
the hormonal chaos,
the days I could barely stand upright—
they needed proof after proof
before they'd believe
I needed relief.

Eventually I stopped
taking the little pills,
and started listening.
Not just to doctors—
but to my body.

What I've learned:
Healing is not a one-size-fits-all solution.
Especially for endometriosis.
It's medical.

It's emotional.
It's energetic.

Somatic healing,
energy work,
deep mind-body connection.
Huge progress.
Also?
Hormonal support that doesn't bully your system
into submission.

Finding the right supplements changed everything:
my energy,
my inflammation,
my hope.

And then there are moments
where my body reacts to pain
that isn't even mine.

Case in point:
I recently learned
I have empathetic ovaries.
Yes—apparently that's a thing.
I was listening to an audiobook,
a memoir threaded with sexual assault,
and my ovaries folded in
like they were filing for early retirement.
A deep ache.
A sharp twist.
A full-body "absolutely not."

Here's the scoop with bodies like mine:

when you've lived years
in chronic pelvic pain—
endo, fibroids, hormonal chaos,
fight-or-flight on speed dial—
your nervous system becomes
a finely tuned alarm system.

It recognizes threat
even when the threat
is only a story.
It contracts in empathy,
in memory,
in warning.
Because the body doesn't just remember
its own trauma—
it remembers patterns.
It echoes old wounds
when it hears new ones.

It's not weakness.
It's wiring.
It's protection dressed as pain.
It's the body saying,
I've seen this shape before.
And I'm not letting you walk through it alone.

Excision surgery is on the table.
But so is trust.
And I'm choosing trust.

To anyone with endo—
I see you.
Your pain is real.

Don't stop fighting for better care.

From 2006 to 2008,
I lived in a body
that flared without warning.
Optical migraines.
Daily chronic headaches.
Hives from head to torso on occasion
that left me unrecognizable.

I became a regular at the ER,
a cocktail away from calm:
epinephrine, benadryl, prednisone—
then sleep it off and start again.

They tried everything:
facet shots to numb the chaos,
nerve blocks to intercept the pain,
hypnosis to unhook the mind from the body,
acupuncture to redirect the current.

Doctor after doctor,
nearly $30,000 out of pocket.
Tests, meds, travel, specialists,
and still—no answers.

And then—
a lump in my breast.
Biopsy scheduled.
Worry stacked on worry.
The unknown pressed in
from every direction.

All while raising
a three-year-old
and a five-year-old—
two bright, beautiful reasons
to keep pretending I was okay.

Honestly?
If I were a horse,
they'd have put me down by now.
But I'm not a horse.
I'm a woman who keeps showing up
despite the odds.

If sarcasm cured inflammation,
I'd be the healthiest woman alive.

The local news station even did a story,
and suddenly every self-proclaimed healer
within a tri-county radius
showed up at my metaphorical doorstep
with potions, powders,
and a whole lot of confidence.

I tried a few.
Most left me more tired than treated.
Then a young physical therapist
just starting out
specializing in women's pelvic pain
looked where no one else had:
down.

My pelvic area was out of alignment—
post-birth,

post-chaos,
post everything.

She said my body was like a house of cards.
Everyone kept focusing on the attic
when it was the basement that collapsed.

A few sessions.
A few exercises I still do today.
And the migraines?
Mostly gone.
Now I just get the occasional optical aura
and the hangover that follows.

I wish I had my Trailblazing Communications Program back
then.
Would've saved money,
energy,
sanity.
That $30K didn't even include missed work.

Then there's the body pain:
neck, shoulders, back,
knees, feet,
even my hands some days.
Functional and somatic movement,
plus an anti-inflammatory diet—
thank you, Coach Tiff—
have been lifesavers.

Chronic pain has robbed years from my life.
Stolen joy.
Hijacked dreams.

But not anymore.
Now, I say I'm aging backward.
Reclaiming what I lost.
And fiercely protecting what I have left.

Because I'm not just healing—
I'm rebuilding.
Not just surviving—
but soaring.
This body?
It's not a graveyard of what's been taken.
It's a monument to what I've overcome.
And from the fire,
I rise.

The Body Remembers—and So Do You Playlist:

"Save Me" – Jelly Roll
"Warrior" – Demi Lovato
"Bird Set Free" – Sia

The Body Remembers—and So Do You Reflection:

What pain have you been told to ignore, minimize, or push through?

How have you reclaimed even a single piece of your health or wholeness?

When was the last time you truly listened to your body—and what did it say?

What would it look like to befriend your body instead of battling it?

What does rising look like for you, today?
Write it out.
Say it loud.

Track 16 Birthdays and Graduations and Weddings and Babies, Oh My

May 4, 2002.
A date you'd think I'd never forget.

A day stacked with
everything good,
everything grown-up,
everything that said
you made it.

I walked across the stage
in a cap and gown with my masters degree
carrying a baby in my belly
and a ring on my finger.

My birthday.
My graduation.
My baby shower.
My wedding shower.

One day.
All of it.

A Hallmark hurricane of milestones.
And yet—
not one picture.
Not one I can find.
Not one that found me.

I know I was celebrated.
Cards.
Cake.
Congratulatory hugs
from people who meant well.

But I've searched
for proof I was actually there—
really seen
in the whirlwind of it all—
and I keep coming up blank.

You'd think it would be framed somewhere.
That I'd have something to hold onto—
besides the ache.

But some moments are like that.
Loud on the outside.
Hollow in the middle.
A standing ovation
for a woman no one really stopped to look at.

And maybe that's why
this Disc is called Full Volume.

Because now,
finally,
I've turned the mic back on.

Birthdays and Graduations and Weddings and Babies, Oh My Playlist

"Invisible" – Hunter Hayes
"I Am Here" – P!nk

Birthdays and Graduations and Weddings and Babies, Oh My Reflection

Think about a time when everything looked beautiful on the outside—but you felt completely invisible on the inside.

What did that moment teach you about your own needs?

What parts of you went uncelebrated that day?

If you could rewrite that memory from the inside out, what would you change?

Track 17 Ink & Identity

I have tattoos.
Not hidden ones—
but etched reminders,
scattered road signs
on the skin I've grown into.

There's a tramp stamp that says HOT
(in flames, obviously).
Nicole's little sister once squinted at it
and said it spelled "Ho."
And honestly, she wasn't wrong.

There's an octopus swimming between my breasts—
a private metaphor I might one day explain
in a special behind-the-scenes story,
but for now,
it's just between me and the ink.

On my back shoulder:

The Kanji symbol for pearl.
It represents a public speaking talk I used to give,
where PEARL stands for:
Passion, Education, Awesomeness, Resilience, Love.
It still does.

There's a butterfly on my wrist—
not the delicate, fluttery kind you'd expect,
but a bold one.

Built from a brain scan.
Shaped by science.
Colored by courage.

It's modeled after my niece Libby's brain—
a silhouette of schizencephaly,
transformed into wings.

It holds a semicolon too.
Not a mistake.
Not an end.
Pause.
Not period.

Still flying.
Still here.

It stings every time I look at it.
And yet—
it soars.

I got one
at a tattoo fundraiser—

a tiny heart
with three arrows.
For the chosen few,
they said.
But really,
for all of us
learning what it means
to love without condition.

Three arrows
for the third chromosome,
for the extra light
some souls bring.
For the reminder
that different
is divine.

It's the smallest tattoo I have—
but it might be
the loudest one
when you listen
with your heart.

And on my right forearm:
a dandelion scattering charm seeds-
symbols for the people who made me,
saved me,
and still shape me.
The stem spells "Live Differently"
in my wife's handwriting—
a quiet vow I carry everywhere.

The seeds...

A soccer ball for Nicole,
Hall of Fame, All-American,
Goal-scoring soul.

A chess piece for Nickolas,
the boy who could outthink any board.

A track shoe for Nathan—
faster than fear,
stronger than circumstance,
All-American in every way that counts.

A compass rose for Scout.
She was still too small
to show me who she was—
but I knew she'd always guide me home.

And a paw print for Buddy,
who reminded me,
every single day,
what unconditional really means.

I wear my story in ink and initials.

I've had a dozen nicknames:

My uncle Danny has always called me Nickodemus.

My family calls me Cole or Coley.

When I was little, I was Gopher.
You already read all about that one.

Went by Nikkol (with two k's and some sass).
for a short chapter in college.

I was Nikki only in Pierre, SD
and to one of my bosses.
He once told me
"Nikki, put your ego in your back pocket."

I've been folding and unfolding that line
in the back pocket
of every pair of pants since.

Some days I wear it like armor.
Some days I forget it's even there.

But it's always stitched in—
just enough reminder
to check myself
before I puff up or spiral out.

I've even been called a Rainmaker—
the kind who makes things happen,
brings the spark,
turns dry seasons
into possibility.

And The Alchemist—
the kind who turns pain into purpose,
chaos into clarity,
words into movement.

And Dreamweaver—
the kind who sees what isn't yet,

pulls thread from the unseen,
and spins it into something real.

But my favorite name?
Since the first time I heard it—
has always been Mom.

Mom to three kids across two decades,
in diapers and dorm rooms,
with scraped knees and scholarship letters.
Mom with snacks,
and solutions,
and silent prayers.

That name—
that role—
is the tattoo on my soul.

My name has been hyphenated,
unhyphenated,
reclaimed.

Nicole and I kept our maiden names—
because sharing a life is one thing,
but sharing a name at the DMV
is a test no marriage needs.

Ink is just the surface.
Identity runs deeper.
And mine?
It's stitched in skin,
etched in memory,
and finally,

finally
worn without apology.

I've worn names
and I've worn ink—
both chosen,
both earned.

Ink & Identity Playlist

"The Tattooed Heart" – Ariana Grande

Ink & Identity Reflection

What stories live on your skin—or your shelves, or your silence?

What names have you worn—and which ones did you not choose?

How have they shaped you? Which ones still fit?

What symbol would you get tattooed to represent who you are now?

Is there a quote, phrase, or line that lives in your "back pocket"?

The thing that shows up right when you need it?

Track 18 Names That Change You

I've worn a lot of titles in my life—
coach, teacher, professor, wife, writer.
But the one that changed me most
was only three letters long.

Mom.

They call me Mom.
And each of them
gave that name
a different meaning.

Nick.

3/14/02.
The first time I wrote "Love Mom"
in a journal I started just for him—
one month after I found out I was pregnant.

He tried to come six weeks early—
impatient from the start.

They gave me shots to stop the contractions,
steroids to help his lungs grow faster,
and sent me home on bed rest.

We were only halfway through our Lamaze classes.
I remember crying because I wasn't ready—
We didn't even have a car seat yet.

I made it a week and a half.
And then it was time.

I pushed so hard
I had to stop pushing—
his heart rate dropped,
his tiny lungs forgot how to breathe.

And then he came.
My Gerber baby.
That's what everyone—
even strangers—
called him when they saw him.

I read to him nonstop every day
and sang "Your Song" on repeat.
I loved breathing in his sweet air—
like every inhale
was proof he was here.

Two years later,
he shook hands with the governor at his inauguration

and said, "Hi, John Hoeven—where's George Bush?"

Confidence was his first language.
He's always had
the quiet certainty
of someone who would one day
be both engineer and president.

Even as a little boy,
he wanted to understand how everything worked—
to take apart, rebuild, improve.
He asked questions like an engineer
and thought like a leader.

He used to track how many books he read each month,
how many hours of tennis
each pair of shoes had played.
He journaled in code,
could solve a Rubik's Cube in under a minute
without looking,
and played chess blindfolded—
because seeing the board
wasn't challenging enough.

Now he's an engineer—
Working on Apache helicopters.

He's the kid who never needed much direction—
just space to think,
room to build,
and a mom who'd listen
when he was ready to talk.

My Bubba Boy.
My first everything.
The one who taught me
that love can be methodical,
steady,
and quietly brilliant.

Nate.

With Nate,
I went into labor at 2 a.m.
and didn't hold him until twenty hours later.

The doctor kept leaving—
checking on her kids' State Track meet races
between checking on me.
Running between the meet and my finish line.

I was the first mom to check in
and the last to deliver.
Every time another baby was born,
a lullaby charm rang overhead—
a reminder that I was still waiting.

He came during track season,
watched the Olympics
before he turned three months,
and won his first race
before he was even one—
the Diaper Dash.
He's been chasing finish lines ever since.

Grew up on Turtle Power and resilience.

When he was little,
he always said he wanted to be
a Teenage Mutant Ninja Turtle
when he grew up.

I had him on a Saturday,
went back to work Tuesday
(only because Monday was Memorial Day),
and played softball that Thursday.

Pretty sure I lost my uterus
somewhere between first and second base.

Second child.
Fewer pictures.
More grit.

But this boy—
this heart-on-his-sleeve boy—
came into the world
to teach me tenderness.
He was my feeler.
My sweetheart.
The one who noticed
when I was too quiet,
too tired,
too "I'm fine."

He'd crawl into my lap
without a word—
just knowing I needed it.
He could read a room before he could read a book,
and somehow always knew

how to soften its edges.

When he was seventeen,
we learned his heart
was literally beating too fast—
electrical storms firing
where peace should have been.
He needed an ablation.
I watched monitors and machines
and whispered prayers
to every corner of the hospital
until his rhythm came back steady.

He woke up with his sly smile,
making jokes about the heart monitor—
like even in pain,
He had to make everyone else comfortable.

That's Nate.
Big-hearted in every sense.

When he loves,
He loves completely.
When he hurts,
he feels it all.
And when he runs—
God, when he runs—
I see just how strong he really is.

My Nate.
My feeler.
My sweetheart.
The one who carries both his heart and mine—

and somehow makes them stronger
every time they beat.

I thought I'd learned patience by then.
Turns out motherhood keeps enrolling you in the same class,
just with different teachers.

They don't tell you
how loud two little boys can be
when you're already late for a softball game.

Opening night of McQuades—
the world's largest charity softball tournament.
I was the team sponsor, the manager,
the second basewoman, the clean up batter.
The busy mom with two kids and twelve gloves.

They were fighting with squirt guns,
laughing, shouting.
I told them to stop.
Told them again.
Then I stomped their squirt guns—
right there in front of everyone.
Their eyes.
My friends' eyes.
All of them were wide with surprise.

Did I stomp on their dreams that day?
Maybe.
But I was doing it all—
daycare pickups,
dinners,
cleats,

schedules.
I was angry.
Tired.
Trying.

Now I laugh,
Trying to parent Scout with "gentle" everything.

Back then,
We had commercials for The Total Transformation System.

Now it's deep breaths and affirmations.
Different decade.
Different tools.
Same love.
Still learning.

One summer,
we went canoeing down the Crow Wing River in Minnesota—
the same trip I'd taken with my science club in junior high, and
dreamt of taking my own kids to one day.

It was half magic, half meltdown.
I pushed the canoes out
and sank knee-deep in mud.
"I SAID, MY FOOT IS STUCK"
became family legend.

We camped with mosquitoes
the size of hummingbirds
and camping neighbors who thought fireworks
were a personality trait.

We still saw a bear.
We still laughed.
Nicole, Buddy, and I in one canoe—
the boys in another.
We raced.
We tipped.
Everything soaked.
And somehow,
it was still perfect.

That's the thing about motherhood—
half the time,
you're knee-deep in mud.
The other half,
you're making memories
they'll tell their kids.

I've written in diaries
to my boys for years.
Words I hope they'll one day read
and understand the woman
behind the title.

Years later,
I asked them questions
from a Facebook trend.
When Nick got to,
"What makes Mom sad?"
he didn't even think.
"When she feels like she's not needed or appreciated," he said.

And he was right.
Maybe it's something

I absorbed before I was born—
my mom's thoughts
when she had me so young.

Maybe it's just the echo
of always needing to matter.
But being their mom
has been both my purpose
and my healing.

They needed me.
And I needed them
to remind me
I was worth being needed.

They call me Mom—
and some days
that still feels like
the most sacred title
I'll ever earn.

It's messy.
It's holy.
It's loud and quiet
and full of second chances.

It's the reason I stayed.
The reason I became.
The reason
this story
exists at all.

Names That Change You Playlist

"You are the Reason" – Calum Scott
"You'll Be in My Heart" – Phil Collins
"Your Song" – Ewan McGregor

Names That Change You Reflection

You've had titles—
maybe dozens of them.
But which one changed you?

The one that taught you patience, or presence, or surrender?

Think of the names you've carried—
the ones you were given,
the ones you earned,
the ones you outgrew.

Then ask yourself:
What name do I answer to now?

And what name do I still need to grow into?

Write about the moment you realized "Mom" (or your own sacred title)
wasn't just something they called you—
it was something you became.

Track 19 Beautiful Strong

Four years.
Seven tries.
And more closed doors than I can count.

A delayed sperm delivery that made us miss our "window."
A global donor shortage.
(Thank you, COVID.)
And the clock tapping its foot at us
like it had somewhere better to be.

Each failed attempt felt heavier.
The injections.
The timing.
The hope that kept whispering,
maybe this time.

Our house looked like a science experiment.
Our hearts felt like one too.
There were early mornings of blood draws,

afternoons of hormones and headaches,
and nights when I'd stare at the ceiling
counting everything we'd already given—
time, money, pieces of ourselves—
for a maybe.

IVF isn't for the faint.
It's for the ones who love
before there's anything to hold.

By the time Scout came along,
I was old enough (49) for the nurse at our first appointment
to smile and say,
"Are you the grandma?"

"GrandmaMom," I joked—
but it stung.

Maybe that's why
I worked so hard—
harder than I ever had—
to rebuild my body
and rewire my mind.

I trained.
I meditated.
I visualized the kind of mother I wanted her to know—
one who moved,
breathed,
and believed in her own strength.

GrandmaMom was tough on me,
reminding me that strength looks like showing up—

even when it hurts.

And I promised myself
my daughter would only know
a healthy version of me.

Somewhere along the way,
I stopped chasing youth
and started reclaiming it.
I swear I'm aging backwards—
every cell rewinding
to match the woman I was always meant to be
before the world told me who to become.

Scout came early too.

Nicole wasn't looking right,
and I asked our doctor to run extra tests.
Two hours later,
We were told to come back—
We were having a baby that day.

Nicole pushed hard.
Sixty-seven times.
(I know because I made tally marks.)

At first, it was just us and a couple of nurses.
Then the doctor joined.
Then suddenly, ten of us filled the room—
and the sound left it.

No cry.
No breath.

Only silence,
and the sound of professionals
doing what they do when everything's on the line.

They whisked her to the warmer.
Twenty seconds old
and already fighting for her life.

I watched through tears
as they dried her,
suctioned blood from her tiny mouth,
pressed air into lungs
that didn't yet know how to open.

They called out her stats—
heart rate climbing,
oxygen rising—
and I exhaled a prayer
I didn't know I'd been holding.

I never got to cut the cord.
One minute I was counting pushes,
the next, she was across the room—
tiny, silent, surrounded by angels in scrubs.

That invisible thread between us
wasn't mine to sever.
It was theirs to save.

They asked me if I wanted to cut the cord after she was already
in the warmer
but I had no clue what was going on.
In a blur of voices and beeping and prayer,

I cut what was left of the cord.

Nicole drifted in and out.
She wouldn't really come back for days.
I almost lost her too.

I thought I was going home without either of them.

Nicole's body had gone through hell.
They started magnesium to calm her system,
a blood transfusion to bring her color back,
Lasix to drain the fluid that refused to let go.

She even had one-on-one care for a full day—
the kind of attention you don't see anymore,
not even in the ICU.

Bag after bag.
Drip after drip.
Machines humming like a lullaby
for a mother who gave everything
to bring another into the world.

I used to think giving birth was hard—
but nothing compared to this.
The helplessness.
The watching and waiting.
The realization that sometimes
all you can do
is breathe,
pray,
and trust the ones trying to save
the people you love most.

Weeks later,
I opened our MyChart
to learn what my body hadn't let my mind understand that day.
This is what it said—
their language, our miracle:

Clinical Team Notes:

Pt brought to pre-warmed panda warmer at aprox 20 seconds
of age, after cord cut.
No respiratory effort, limp, dried and stimulated, orally
suctioned for mod bloody secretions, PPV with T-piece peep 4
at 21% FiO2 per Mel RRT, wet blankets removed, stimulating
pt.
1240: PPV with T-piece peep 4 per Mel RRT increased FiO2
to 30%., oximeter applied, continue to stimulate pt.
1241 and 45 seconds: PPV paused, occasional respiratory
effort, pinking up slowly, oral pharynx suctioned for mod
amount of bloody secretions. PPV resumed per Mel RRT. Wet
blankets removed again.
1242: PPV with peep 4 and 30% continued per Mel RRT.1242
and 30 seconds, Erica NNP and Dr. Morgan-Harris at bedside,
Oximeter 69% HR 145.
1243 and 15 seconds: Dr. Morgan-Harris removed PPV, pt has
spont resp., lung sounds clearing, orally suctioned for small
bloody secretions.
1243 and 20 seconds: HR 149, sat 64 on room air
1243 and 35 seconds: Dr. Morgan-Harris herself resumes
CPAP Peep 4, FiO2 increased to 40% sat 70.
1245 and 45 seconds: Dr. Morgan-Harris stops CPAP. Sats 88,
HR 190
1246: Stomach suction for mod amount bloody secretions.
1247: HR 171 sat 88-90 on Room Air.

1249: HR 200 sat 98, Dr. Harris speaking to moms.
1251: pt wrapped in 3 warm blankets with hat on, given to
Mom - Nicole (OB pt) to hold.
1255: Pt placed in crib and transported to NICU 608 mom
(non OB pt) accompanied to NICU. Pt has two ID bands on,
one on arm and one on leg.
1300: report given to Katarina RN

During that blur of time,
what came to me in the moment
wasn't a number.
It was a song.

For months,
I'd been playing her the Rockabye Baby version of "Yellow" by
Coldplay.

Every night.
Every morning.
A melody she already knew
from inside Nicole.

And when the room turned into a command center,
when my daughter hadn't made a sound,
I pressed play.

A song about stars and devotion filled the room.
About light meant just for her.

I swear she heard it.
And just like that—
color.

A flicker.
A gasp.
The smallest cry
with the biggest meaning.

At 12:51,
they placed her in Nicole's arms—
warm, pink, breathing, alive.

At 12:55,
I followed her tiny crib to the NICU,
two ID bands glinting like constellations.

A couple years later, we'd face another kind of fight—
the one on paper.
Even though my name was listed as the "father" on her birth
certificate,
I still had to legally adopt her.

Because love isn't always enough
in the political climate we live in.
I held the same baby I'd prayed for,
the one whose first breath came with a song,
and had to prove
I was her mother.

The day she was born I called her Beautiful—
and she gave me the side-eye.
So I said, fine—
"Beautiful Strong."
And she smiled.

Because she is.

Because we are.

Because sometimes love needs
a chart,
a choir of miracle workers,
and a song
to find its way into the world.

Beautiful Strong Playlist

"Daughter" – Sleeping at Last
"Yellow" – Rockabye Baby
"I Get to Love You" – Ruelle
"Girls" – Rachel Platten
"Trustfall" – P!NK (Five minutes before active labor kicked in,
we were watching P!NK on the Today Show. This song looped
in my head through the entire delivery—the soundtrack to the
moment she arrived. Scout's first anthem.)

Beautiful Strong Reflection

There are moments in life when strength doesn't look like
movement.
It looks like stillness.
Like standing in a room full of noise
and choosing to keep breathing.

Think about a time when you felt powerless—
when love or life or healing was out of your hands.

What carried you through it?

A person? A song? A whisper of hope you couldn't explain?

Write about the moment something shifted.
When you realized strength isn't always in the doing—
sometimes it's in the being.

Then ask yourself:
What part of me is trying to be born now?
And what song—literal or metaphorical—will I play to help it
find its breath?

Track 20 Wish Granter

Before I was a mom,
taught classes,
built businesses,
or stood on stages—
I granted wishes.

For over twenty years, I volunteered with Make-A-Wish,
and served on the board.
Even became vice chair.
But the position that meant the most?
Wish Granter.

It started with a dance.
A little girl named Autumn—five years old,
vision in only one eye,
due to the pressure from her brain tumor.
Her walker steadying her bowed tibia—
tugged me onto the dance floor
at a fundraising event.

She requested "Twinkle Twinkle"
and Shania Twain's "Man! I Feel Like a Woman"—
Song after song
We danced like the world was ours.

"Where do I sign up?" I'd asked—
not realizing that question
was the beginning of a lifetime
of saying yes to magic.

I still have a letter she typed for me.
Her mom translated the gibberish.
It was perfect.

I couldn't tell you how many wishes I've granted.
Every time I try to count,
I get distracted by the memories.
The faces. The laughter.
The ones I thought I forgot come rushing back.

But I remember my first:
Bobby. Four years old.
It was right after 9/11,
and his family boarded the first flight allowed out.

My wish partner and I,
We dressed as Mickey and Minnie to meet him at the airport.
I called ahead.
However, the airport administration didn't tell the National
Guard.
We were met by soldiers with guns drawn—
until we explained,
then we took photos

with soldiers grinning beside cartoon ears.

When Bobby got home,
he invited me over
to show me pictures
and return the money they hadn't spent—
so it could go to the next wish family.
That's who wish kids are.
Always thinking of others.

When we met with the kids
we always played the "wish game":
If you could go anywhere, where?
Meet anyone—who?
Have anything—what?
Be anything—what would you become?
Once they answer which one they want the most -
It is our job to expand and enhance the experience.

One boy said he wanted flip flops.
I told him to dream bigger buddy.
He wanted to be a firefighter.
He wanted to go to Disney,
To meet all the characters he watched on TV.

So I called the local fire department.
They picked him up at 5 a.m.
to take him to the airport.
He wailed the siren
all the way across town
on his way to meet all his Disney friends.

Some of the families stay in your life.

Some shape it.
There was a teen with a fierce attitude
and a heart full of gratitude.
He and his mom are why we—
those of us choosing to live differently—
say, "Be grateful. Have faith."
They're an instrumental part of why
the Oola message became a movement.

After my boys were born,
granting wishes got harder—
but I didn't stop.
Sometimes they'd send a toy
with me to pass along.
A car. A stuffed animal. A note in crayon.

Empathy,
taught through little hands
who'd never met the kids
but knew the power of giving.

Two decades later,
I still can't tell you how many wishes I was a part of.
But I can tell you what it gave me:
proof that time is sacred,
that joy should never be taken for granted,
that moments matter more than milestones,
and that when life hands you the chance
to be part of someone's magic—
you take it.
Every time.

Wish Granter Playlist

"Man! I Feel Like a Woman!" – Shania Twain
"My Wish" – Rascall Flatts

Wish Granter Reflection

What's the most magical experience you've ever had that didn't involve money or status—just connection?

When was the last time you said yes to something that changed your life before you even realized it?

If you had to play the "wish game" right now—go anywhere, meet anyone, have anything, be anything—what would your answers be? Which one would you pick?

Who in your life has reminded you of what really matters? Have you told them?

What could you do this week to be someone else's "wish granter," even in a small way?

Track 21 Confident Enough to Flap – Lessons in joy, identity, and the sacredness of the Me File.

I've helped set three world records.
Not the kind that end in medals—
but the kind that live on local news reels
and inside jokes.

The first?
Most people simultaneously making snow angels.
North Dakota pride, baby.

The second?
World's longest chicken dance.
Yes. I flapped. I spun. I committed.

The third?
World's longest twist.
Chubby Checker would've been proud.

I played Ms. Monopoly

for the Junior Achievement fundraiser.
Every year, I dressed the part.
Not as a joke.
With full sincerity.
I wore the top hat,
carried the cane,
ran the auction.
I was all in—banker and all.

For three years,
I wrote a monthly column for The City Magazine:
You've Come a Long Way, Baby.
And oh, have I.

I've always loved learning.
I'm the sponge you can't fill.
It didn't kick in until I was 23 or so—
and then again in 2006
when I became obsessed
with becoming a better person.

One year I read over 100 books.
Back in high school? Just *Lord of the Flies*.
In college? *Man's Search for Meaning*.

I didn't love learning until I realized it could change me.

When I would bring friends home from college,
my Grandpa would tell them,
"I went through college—
in one door and out the other."
Many years later,

I'd steal his line and say,
"I went to Harvard."
Same family joke—
just better branding.

My life mission?
Do what you love
in service to those who love what you do.
(Steve Farber. Radical Leap. Credit where credit is due.)

I almost said no to hosting Ethics Day—
newly-out (again),
terrified that being in love with a woman
would somehow disqualify me.

When I told the event coordinator that,
she smiled and said,
"That doesn't matter."
And I could've cried,
because for the first time,
it finally felt like it didn't.

Someone once told me
My confidence is intimidating.
I wish they knew how hard-won it is.

I had to make a list once—
of all my accomplishments.
I was in a low place
and needed reminding.
It helped.

I keep a "Me File"—

not a folder,
a Rubbermaid tote.
It's packed with proof.
Awards, letters of commendation,
notes from judges, students, and strangers.
Photos from championship games
and costume-filled fundraisers.
Programs from keynote speeches,
team rosters, thank-you cards,
and snapshots from nights
when I got to stand in the spotlight.

It's my archive of evidence.
That says I matter
on the days I forget.

One of the things that's pulled me through
over and over
is not forgetting who I've been.

I carry a thousand versions of me.
And sometimes, I dress them up,
give them top hats,
and let them dance.
All of them true.
All of them still here.

Nicole and I joke that we're humble narcissists.
So confident in some places,
so insecure in others.
#Balance.

Somewhere between ink and identity,

ego and ethics,
I stopped apologizing
for being a walking contradiction.
And I just started
showing up as the whole damn parade.

Top hat, twist, Harvard joke and all.
Confident enough to flap.
Quiet enough to hear my own knowing.
Loud enough to never lose her again.

Confident Enough to Flap Playlist

"Chicken Dance"
"Glorious" – Macklemore ft. Skylar Grey

Confident Enough to Flap Reflection

Everyone has a Me File.
For some, it's a literal box.
For others, it's a mental highlight reel they forget to replay.

Reflect on a few of these questions (or write them down somewhere you'll see when doubt creeps in):

What's one accomplishment I rarely celebrate but absolutely
should?

What version of me helped me survive a season I thought I
wouldn't?

What artifact, letter, or moment would I put in my own "Me File"?

Now finish this sentence:
"The most unapologetically me moment I've ever had was when I..."
(Don't overthink. Just flap.)

Track 22 Pink Slips & Bird Sh*t

Because apparently, getting dumped on by birds and employers is a theme. What job loss taught me about identity, grit, and showing up anyway).

I've been sh*t on—
literally and professionally.

Once by a bird on the way to a parade,
once mid-sentence under a tree,
and more times than I can count
by companies that closed the doors
without warning,
without reason,
without apology.

Jobs I showed up for with my full self.
Jobs I lost without fault.

Job #1: The Education Agent

I was four months pregnant
with my youngest son
when they told us the company was closing.

No warning.
No severance.
Not even pay owed.
Just—doors shut.

No job.
No plan.
No one calling back.

I thought I'd bounce back fast.
I didn't.

Weeks turned to months,
and nothing came.

I spiraled.
Started to believe
maybe I wasn't worth hiring.
Maybe I wasn't as good as I thought.

But I refused to stay stuck.
So I pulled up my big-girl panties—
(and they were maternity-sized,
so they really meant business)—
and marketed the hell out of myself.

That's when my public speaking life took off.

From the ashes of rejection,
I started using my voice.
And people listened.

Job #2: The Nonprofit That Ghosted Me

I landed a role
running a nonprofit for the working poor.
It felt aligned—heart-forward, community-centered.

I went to pick up the manuals.
Told them I was due in June.
I just needed a few days off. That's all.

When I got home,
there was a message on the machine.
They had "gone a different direction."
They wanted the manuals back.

No meeting.
No conversation.
Just a clean cut.
Because I was pregnant.
And they couldn't say that,
but we both knew.

That was the first time
my motherhood disqualified me
before I could even start.

A month later,
a respected ad agency hired me.
I didn't tell them I was pregnant for weeks.

I was scared.

But when I did—
they didn't flinch.
They told me to take the time I needed.
That kind of grace
sticks with you forever.

Job #3: The One That Changed the Rules

Nine years I gave them.
Heart, hustle, weekends, wins.
Then a new dean came in—
with a new vision
that didn't include me.

They rewrote the job description
to require a doctorate,
knowing I didn't have one.
Even my boss was blindsided.
I was replaced.

And the person after me?
Didn't even last a semester.
But the damage was done.

I stopped working there in 2010.
And didn't start feeling like myself again
until 2021.

That one cut deep.
Not because I lost a job—
but because I lost a version of myself

I had worked so hard to become.

Job #4 & 5: The Ones That Closed

Marketing. Career Counseling.
Different companies, same story.
Doors closed.
Locations gone.
Nothing to do with performance—
everything to do with survival.

I used to take it personally.
Now I understand
it was just business.
But when you pour your soul into work
and it disappears overnight,
it still feels personal.

The Unspoken Ones

And then—
there were a few more.
Jobs I barely mention
because I barely made it through.

On paper they looked fine.
In practice, they were mind games.
There's no easy way to explain
what it feels like to be
professionally gaslit
by someone with charm, power,
and zero accountability.

Those roles didn't end with a pink slip—
They ended with me choosing myself.
Even when I didn't yet know
what I was choosing myself for.

Through all of it—
there was one constant.
"Bring on the Rain" by Jo Dee Messina.
I'd blast it in the car,
and sing like it she wrote it just for me—
cracked voice and all,
crying behind the wheel,
belting through the pain.

Job loss has a way
of making you question your worth—
especially when it happens
over
and over
again.

Sometimes,
it feels like a death
with no funeral.
You grieve the version of you
that used to matter to someone.
And no matter how strong you are—
when your role, your purpose,
is handed to the friend of the new hire,
you bleed a little.

But every ending
was actually a turning point.

And every time I got let go,
I let go of something too:
the need to prove,
the fear of starting over,
the lie that my value
was tied to someone else's title.

But every no
pushed me to say yes
to something of my own.
Turns out,
getting sh*t on
wasn't a sign of failure.

It was a cosmic reset.
A push.
A clearing.
A divine nudge saying:
"You were never meant to play small in someone else's box."

Pink Slips & Bird Sh*t Playlist

"Bring on the Rain" – Jo Dee Messina
"Fight Song" – Rachel Platten

Pink Slips & Bird Sh*t Reflection

Think back to a time you were let go—
from a job, a role, a title, or a version of yourself you'd worked
hard to earn.

What did you believe about yourself in the aftermath?

What did you let go of in the process—besides the job?

What hidden opportunity, gift, or grit came forward that may never have surfaced otherwise?

Now, write a permission slip to your past self.

Finish this sentence:
"Even though they let you go, you were never meant to stay because..."

Track 23 High-Strung & Half-Baked

I always joke that I wish I had a pothead mentality.
Laid-back.
Chill.
One with the couch and the munchies.

Instead, I'm high-strung.
Over-wound.
Wired like a raccoon on espresso.

When we went to Vancouver for the World Cup,
Nicole and I were already a few adventures in—
but this one still stands out
as the trip where she got to see
just how high-strung
her girlfriend really was.

I made it a mission—
a spiritual quest—

to finally try pot like a grown-up.
To redeem that one terrible
college experience.

We drove down to Seattle.
Picked up some edible cookies.
I ate half of one
somewhere between anticipation and Pike Place.

When it hit—
I was a half-baked sugar cookie
without a pan,
melting through the wire rack.

Hungry, but unable to eat.
Barely alert, utterly useless.

I watched Nicole and her sister Summer ride the Ferris wheel
while I sat clutching my purse
like it was my firstborn,
absolutely convinced someone could
sense my vulnerability.

I wrapped it around my neck and arms—
cradled it like a baby bear—
because I'd assisted with
one too many situational-awareness classes
from Pretty Loaded.

Later, we drove into the absolute middle of nowhere.

Pot was legal in Washington,

but...
Couldn't smoke in the hotel.
Couldn't smoke in the rental.
Definitely couldn't smoke in public.

So we found a stretch of trees
beside a quiet lake,
where the wind wouldn't tell
and the trees wouldn't judge.

I finally smoked the joint
I'd made such a big deal about.
And when I coughed,
my lung nearly skipped across the lake
like a perfect flat rock.

Honestly—
that might've been
the moment she realized
this was a lifetime subscription to chaos
and signed up anyway.

A few years later,
we went to Denver
for a "medical study"
to see if I should apply for a medical-marijuana card
to help with chronic pain.

The answer was yes.
Still is.
But I haven't applied.

Not sure if I'm afraid of

losing control,
being judged,
or simply needing to depend on something.

I still laugh when I tell these stories.

But behind the humor is the truth:
I've built a life around being the strong one.

So the idea of letting go—
even just enough to feel better—
still feels like
giving something up.
Even now.

High-Strung & Half-Baked Playlist

"Let Go" – Frou Frou
"Control" – Zoe Wees
"Hold On" – Wilson Phillips

High-Strung & Half-Baked Reflection

Where in your life do you feel the need to "hold it together" at all costs?

What are you afraid might happen if you didn't?

What does "letting go" look like for you—not as a concept, but as a practice?
Be honest. Be gentle.

Is there something you've avoided because it means admitting you need relief?

What if needing help was not weakness, but wisdom?

Track 24 Nicole.Morrison2.0

After I finished coaching with Tiff,
I changed my social handles to @Nicole.Morrison2.0.

It wasn't just a username.
It was a declaration.

A reminder
that I could update my operating system
without deleting the original code.

One moment stands out that built this shift—
a dinner with Tiff
during the Coaching intensive in California.

I ordered a drink.
Took one sip.
Didn't like it.

Tiff said, "Send it back."

I shook my head. "No, it's okay."

She leaned in a little and said,
"No, it's not."

I told her I didn't want them to throw it away.

She looked at me steady and sharp,
and said,
"So you're fine drinking something you don't even want—
because you think you're worth less than trash?"

I just sat there.

Then I sent it back.

That small act—
sending back the drink—
rippled through everything.

It became a symbol of self-advocacy—
a quiet revolution in a single motion.

Even now, I find myself saying
"Send it back,"
when I start to settle.

It's become a shorthand
for boundaries, truth,
and choosing what serves me
without guilt.

I'm proud of how I now honor

both Little Nicole and Present-Day Nicole—
meeting their needs
with love and intention.

I've shifted
out of survival mode
into alignment,
flow,
and intentionality.

A few days after my coaching wrapped with Tiff,
I was on a call with my friend Marilyn.

In five minutes,
she helped me see
the vision for this book.
She saw a pink flower
standing in a wheat field.
She heard "Don't Stop Believin'."
She said my purpose
was to remove judgment from the world—
to help people tell their stories
with authenticity.

And here we are.
Nicole.Morrison2.0
wasn't a rebrand.
It was a rebirth.
One sip,
one sentence,
one truth at a time.

Nicole.Morrison2.0 Playlist

"Breakaway" – Kelly Clarkson
"Brand New" – Ben Rector

Nicole.Morrison2.0 Reflection

When was the last time you settled for something you didn't
actually want—because it felt easier than speaking up?

What would "sending it back" look like in your life right now?
A decision? A boundary? A belief?

How can you honor both your younger self and your present
self—
not by choosing one over the other,
but by letting them grow together?

What part of you is ready for an update—
not to erase who you were,
but to expand who you've become?

Track 25 That Day

(This is a hidden track. The kind you only find if you let the album play past the silence.)

Suicide is so cruel.
It's brutal in ways that logic can't touch.
If you've never thought about it—
not once—
you are so f'ing lucky.

It doesn't always look like a plan.
It doesn't always come with a note.
It doesn't always mean you want to die.

Sometimes,
you just can't figure out
how to keep living.

I was strong.
Happy-looking.

Capable.
A mom.
An educator.
A climber of mountains.
A woman who helped teenagers plan their futures during the
day, and couldn't imagine her own by night.
A woman who smiled in public
and dissolved in private.

And still—
there I was,
in a $200-a-month apartment in Phoenix, Arizona.

Rooming with a woman in her 60s.
Bottles of pills.
And a whisper of a goodbye
only I could hear.

She took the living room.
I had the bedroom.
She was always at the nursing home with her mom.
(That's why I was there—to help pay her mom's nursing home
expenses).

So it was mostly just me and the silence.
Or the soft hiss of a white-noise website
I used to muffle the loneliness
and keep the quiet from swallowing me whole at night.

My job was at a fancy prep school, the kind where the students'
car floor mats cost more than my tiny Vercedes
(aka Nissan Versa).

I was surrounded by privilege by day, but barely surviving by night.

I chose that apartment because it was cheap.
Phoenix isn't.
But disappearing was.

She had a mountain of medications.
So did I.
And I wasn't worried about mixing them—
I planned to take them all.
Prescription. Over-the-counter.
Whatever I could find.

Maybe they'd work.
Maybe they wouldn't.
Maybe they'd just make me crap my pants
before my heart gave out.

It's funny now.
It wasn't then.

I had felt this way before—
more than once—
but never this close.
Never with a whole plan in place.

Maybe because I was different.
A kind of different not even I had fully embraced.
The kind that made me feel alone,
even in a room full of people.

I was ghosting out of my own life.

No food.
Just MonaVie juice—those purple bottles of false energy.

I was the skinniest I'd been since high school.
Skinny-fat. Hollow.

My parents hadn't talked to me in over a year.
Nicole had dumped me—again.
And my boys?
They seemed just fine without me.

That was the lie that cut the deepest: that no one needed me.
That no one would notice if I was gone.

My only tether was a virtual farm.
Some app the boys liked.
I grew their crops.
Took screenshots of them.
Texted them to their dad to show them.

It was how I still got to be a mom
when I didn't feel like a person.

My bedroom ceiling was covered in paper snowflakes—
Nate made them.
Little cutouts of childhood,
frozen above my bed
like the version of me I was trying to remember.

And then came that morning.

The day I was going to do it.

The screaming.
My roommate—on her knees in the living room,
wailing to God to save her daughter.
She had just gotten a text.
A goodbye.
The same goodbye
I had rehearsed in my head
for weeks.

But instead of taking the pills,
I ran out to her.
I picked up her phone.
We made calls.
Tracked her daughter down.
I told her everything
I wished someone had told me.
And just like that—
the girl who didn't think she mattered
saved a life.

Maybe two.

That's the punchline no one expects.
I was planning to die.
Instead, I became the one saying:
"You're not alone."
"You are needed."
Words I didn't believe yet.
But I spoke them anyway.

That's how I survived.
By accident.
By divine timing.

By being needed
one more time
before I disappeared.

Maybe that was the miracle.
Maybe it was the beginning
of finding my reason.

The day after,
I would call my mom—
for the first time in well over a year.
Two weeks later,
she would fly down to Arizona
and help me move back home.

I never told her.
Just like you—
when she reads this book,
it will be the first time she hears the story.

You don't have to attempt it
to be a suicide survivor.
You just have to live
through the moment
when dying seems like the only mercy.

You have to make it
to the next sunrise.
Even if no one sees it.

You don't have to prove your pain
to validate your healing.
You don't have to justify staying.

You did something brave—
you stayed.
Sometimes survival is the success story.

And if no one else has told you—
let me be the first:
I'm so glad you're still here.

After the storm of that morning,
I climbed a mountain instead.

Piestewa Peak.
I took my time.
No rush.
The kind of slowness
that only comes
after you've already said goodbye in your head.

I sat at the top and read.
I don't remember the book.
But I remember the quiet.
The not-deadness of it all.
The air felt like a second chance
I hadn't asked for.
And then the sun started to set.

No flashlight.
No "dork torch," what we call headlamps.
So I ran.
Half alive.
Half scared.
All adrenaline.

There's a kind of sadness
that doesn't scream.
It seeps.
It hums in your bones
until you don't even notice it's there—
just that you're not.

Not hungry.
Not angry.
Not joyful.
Not needed.
That was the worst part:
not feeling needed.

Like if I disappeared,
the world would just absorb the silence.

Even my name felt like it belonged to someone else—
someone stronger.
Someone who still remembered how to laugh
without checking to see if it was appropriate first.

I wasn't numb.
Actually numb would've been a relief.
I felt everything.
All at once.
Like standing in a house
where every smoke alarm is going off
but there's no fire
and no one else hears it.

People say,
"Why didn't you call someone?"

But who?
I didn't want to be a burden.
Even now—
when people see my strength,
my family,
my success—
they don't see her.
The girl who sat in a paper-snowflake room,
talking to a digital farm,
because it was the only place
she still felt like she mattered.

They see the Table I've built.
They don't always see the floor
I almost disappeared into.

But both are real.

And both significant.

And yet—
If that day had gone the other way—
I would have missed seeing Nickolas
become a National Merit Scholar.
I wouldn't have watched Nathan
fly down Hayward Field
and become a two time national champion.
I wouldn't have married Nicole.
There would be no Scout—
no spitfire redhead calling me Momma M.
No seats saved in the bleachers.
No late-night talks.
No arms around me at Christmas.

Just an empty chair
where I would've been.

If you've ever made it
through the storm alone,
with nothing but your heartbeat
and a maybe—
you're a survivor.

And maybe one day,
like me,
you'll build something beautiful
on top of the ashes
you didn't leave behind.

That Day Playlist

"Rescue" – Lauren Daigle
"Somebody Does" – Tigirlily Gold
"Unsteady" – X Ambassadors
"Ok to Not Be Ok" – Demi Lovato and Marshmello
"Alive" – Sia
"Momma I'm Coming Home" – Ozzy
"You'll Be Ok"– Great Big World

That Day Reader Reflection:

Have you ever survived something in silence?

Not the kind of survival people celebrate—
but the kind you carry quietly.

Think back to a moment you almost gave up.

What pulled you back?
What kept you anchored?
Was it a person?
A whisper?
A responsibility?
A stubborn heartbeat?

Write a letter to the version of you who stayed.
Thank them.

And if you've never written about that day—
whatever it was for you—
maybe today is the day.

You don't have to share it.
But you're allowed to tell it.

Track 26 The Gift - A Voice for the Voiceless

"A voice for the voiceless,"
my friends Tara and Marilyn
would say to me.
It sounded noble—
but vague.
Like something I'd grow into
once I finally did something big enough.

I used to think it was a compliment.
Something people said to fill a card
or validate my passion for inspirational messages.

I was told I had a voice before I ever believed it.
Not a loud one. Not always a certain one.
But one that stayed—even when I didn't use it.

Which is wild, considering
my mom and siblings used to play a game called
"Do you hear anything?"

pretending they couldn't hear me at all.

I wasn't just learning how to speak.
I was learning how to be heard.

I didn't write this book to prove anything.
I wrote it because somewhere along the way,
I realized the gift my grandpa saw
wasn't just my voice.
The gift was the choice
to finally use it.

Long before I translated energy
or wrote words to free it,
I built a radio station
with my friend Stacy.

We called it URL (U Rock Lately) Radio—
a mic, a laptop, a borrowed soundboard,
and a belief that stories deserved to be heard.

People said we wouldn't last two years.
Sixteen years later,
they are still tuning in.

We broadcasted live from the State Fair,
from the Sturgis Motorcycle Rally,
even from Guatemala—
our little station
that could.

We handed people microphones
who'd never had one before.

Famous, not famous—
everyone had a voice
worth turning the volume up for.

By 2017, I let it go—
not the message,
just the machinery.
I needed to take care of myself.

But the work planted a truth
that's still in everything I do:

Sometimes the loudest way to serve the voiceless
is to step back
and listen.

And when I finally put down the mic,
life handed me a different kind of frequency.

I became Miss Libby's caregiver.
My niece.
Born with Schizencephaly—
missing parts of her brain and her corpus callosum.

With that came cerebral palsy,
epilepsy,
respiratory issues, labeled "non-verbal,"
and a body that didn't always follow orders.
But make no mistake:
Libby speaks.

She just doesn't need words.
She communicates in energy,

in presence,
in a stillness so deep
it can echo through your whole nervous system
if you let it.

With the help of Trailblazing Communications—
a gift my friend Tara created,
and Libby and I learned to dance with—
I became her translator.
Not her mouthpiece,
but rather her microphone.

I learned to hear her through stillness,
feel her in frequencies.
I tuned in to her energy
and began hearing
what others couldn't.
We shared those messages with the world on her Facebook
page "The Diary of Miss Libby."

We've kept her out of hospitals
that would've swallowed her whole
because we listened
before things turned to crisis.

Her teachers know.
Her classmates know.
Anyone who truly sees her knows:
She is not silent.
She is fluent
in a language most of the world forgot.

But the truth is—

I needed her more than she needed me.

She needed witnessing.
And I...
I needed her stillness
like oxygen.

I needed
someone who didn't ask me to perform.
Didn't need credentials.
Didn't rush me through the ache.
Libby let me sit in silence
long enough to hear myself again.

Libby didn't ask me to be anything
other than there.

She gave me presence.
She gave me pause.
She gave me purpose that wasn't attached
to success or speaking gigs
or to-do lists
or proving anything at all.

And now,
as our roles begin to shift again,
as I return to being just her Auntie—
not her caregiver,
but her witness—
She sent me a message.
One I didn't hear with my ears,
but felt in my bones:

"You're not abandoning me.
You're releasing what's not yours
to carry alone anymore."

I wept reading it.
Not because it hurt—
but because it healed.

She reminded me
that the belief
"I will always struggle while others float through life with ease"
wasn't just mine—
it was ours.
Inherited.
Threaded into our nervous systems
like a warning.
Like a pact we never meant to sign.

"Don't disappear into duty," she told me.
"Come back into color."
I had forgotten what color looked like
on my own canvas.

I hadn't picked up a paintbrush
or let myself be the art
in years.

She reminded me:
You don't prove love through depletion.
You show it
by becoming whole
and letting them witness your return.

Libby taught me
how to feel safe in stillness.
Now it's my turn
to feel safe in movement.

I've been using my voice
since I was old enough
to stand behind a podium.

Speech club.
Debate tournaments.
Voice of Democracy winner in high school—
despite a teacher who tried to strip me
of that victory
with a whisper of plagiarism.

She was wrong.
But years later,
when I showed up on the news,
she said,
"I always knew Nicole would do great things."

Maybe she saw the fire.
Maybe that's why she pushed.
Maybe those who challenge us
sometimes believe in us the most.

Since 2003,
I've spoken on stages across the country.
Big rooms. Small rooms.
Legislatures and leadership conferences.
Sometimes with a script.
Sometimes with a spark

that wouldn't let me stay in my seat.

Like the day I testified
against North Dakota House Bill 3013.
A bill that tried to legislate
my family
out of legitimacy.

The heart of my testimony that day:

Good afternoon, Chairperson Larsen and members of the
committee...

I told them about my family—
about my wife,
about our sons,
our daughter with her curls and fire,
and how I had to adopt her
just to stay her mother
in the eyes of a system
that didn't see me clearly.

I told them about values.
Community.
Love.
I told them we are good people.
Not less than. Not broken. Not other.

I stood there not just as another speaker,
but as a mom,
as a wife,
as a voice.
And I said:

"Please do not pass a law
that tells our children
their family is worth less than yours."

That's what it means
to be a voice for the voiceless.
Not to speak over them,
but to echo their truth
when the world tries to ignore it.

To make the invisible
unmissable.

To carry their sacred knowing
into rooms they can't physically enter—
but spiritually fill.

To be the voice
that says:
We are here.
We matter.
We will not be silenced.
Because even in their silence,
their heartbeat is thunder.

And maybe this book
is one more voice.
One more mirror.
One more mic drop
in the growing chorus
of stories that refuse to stay silent.

We're living in an era

where silence is being broken
in every corner of society—
but many still don't know how to tell their truth.

My hope is that
Growing Up Happy in a Lonely World
offers more than a story.
It's a gift to anyone
who's ever felt invisible,
broken,
or mislabeled.

This is not just a memoir.
It's a mirror.
A megaphone.
A map.

That it meets people
where they've buried their pain
and shows them how to rise with it—
not in spite of it,
but because of it.

If even one person reads it
and finally feels seen?
Then it's done its job.
And so have I.

Maybe that's what they meant all along.
Not a title—
a transmission.

The Gift - A Voice for the Voiceless Playlist

"Brave" – Ella Henderson
"Roar" – Katy Perry
"For Good" – Gabriel Mann

The Gift - A Voice for the Voiceless Reflection

Where in your life have you built something that others
doubted—and how did it change you when you finally set it
down?

Who (or what) has given you the gift of stillness?

Have you ever mistaken it for stagnation when it was really
safety?

What parts of your truth have gone unspoken—
not because they were untrue, but because they didn't fit the
mold of what others were ready to hear?

Write them down. Let them breathe.

In what ways have you been the voice for someone else?
And in what ways are you still waiting for someone to be the
voice for you?

What would "coming back into color" mean for you right now?
Not metaphorically—what would it look like on your calendar,
your body, your art, your breath?

Track 27 Gratitude
in Full Volume

Before I thank anyone else, I have to start here—
with the lesson that kept finding me no matter how many times
I tried to outrun it.

I used to think loneliness meant something was missing—
a person, a place,
a part of me that never quite caught up.

But now I know it was space—
space for gratitude to take root,
space for joy to find its way back in.
Gratitude taught me how to look at what hurt
and still say" thank you."

For the lessons that came disguised as loss,
for the people who left and the ones who stayed,
for the mirrors that showed me what still needed love.

Happiness didn't arrive with noise or applause.
It arrived quietly—
in the ordinary, holy moments that stitched me back together.

A warm hand.
A toddler's laugh.
A truth finally spoken aloud.

I've learned that happiness isn't the absence of loneliness.
It's the grace that grows inside it.

It's learning to see what's still good,
still here,
still holding you.
That's what this whole book has been about—
the becoming, the unlearning, the remembering.

So yes—this is me,
growing up happy in a lonely world.
Not because it was easy,
but because gratitude turned even the lonely places into light.

To Nicole, the boys, and Scout—
You've been my reason, my reminder, and my rhythm.

You make this world my favorite place to be—
and I hope, through these pages,
I've left a little more light for you to walk in, too.

To Libby—
You've taught me more in your silence
than most people ever will with words.

Thank you for reminding me
that presence is its own kind of voice.

Your light isn't small.
It's quiet, steady, and strong—
like you.

To my sister—
for being there when it felt like no one else was,
for seeing me through the mess and the magic,
for loving me loud when the world went quiet,
and for never once asking me to be anything
other than myself.

To my parents—
You gave me life.
And in your own way,
you gave me stories I was strong enough to survive.
Thank you for both.

To Coach Tiff—
Thank you for seeing through the noise and holding me to a
higher standard when I forgot my own.
For reminding me that success without alignment isn't success
at all.

You coached me to raise my expectations—
in clients, in confidence,
and yes, in cocktails.
For sending back the drink,
and teaching me that excellence isn't extra—it's energy.

You helped me remember
that the way we do one thing
is the way we do everything.

To my people—
my front row, mentors, readers, healers, and believers—
thank you for catching me between chapters.
For the laughter,
the late-night check-ins,
the editing eyes,
and the kind of sacred honesty
that made this book what it is.

To Marilyn—
for sparking the idea and the vision that set this book in motion.
That ten-minute phone call changed everything.
You reminded me what it means to see possibility before it's
real—
and to trust the pull when the story starts whispering.

To the women of The FoundHers Table—
thank you for building and believing
in something that mirrors what I hoped this book would do:
remind women they're not alone,
and that it's safe to take up space.

To my clients and community—
thank you for letting me witness your breakthroughs.
You've helped me live mine.

To every reader who found themselves somewhere in these
pages—

you're the reason this story kept going.
You are the proof
that our voices were never meant to stay silent.

And to the younger me—
thank you for surviving long enough
to tell the story.

Gratitude in Full Volume Playlist

"Thank U" – Alanis Morissette
"Grateful" – Rita Ora
"I Lived" – One Republic

Gratitude in Full Volume Reflection

Take a moment to breathe before you write.
Not to fix or force a silver lining—just to notice what's still steady.

Ask yourself:

What's something I once took for granted that I now see as sacred?

Where has loss or disappointment quietly grown into something beautiful?

Who (or what) still anchors me, even when I forget to say thank you?

Finish this sentence:
"I didn't realize how much it meant until..."

Let your answer be messy, simple, or small.
Gratitude doesn't need to be profound.
It just needs to be felt.

Bonus Track Why This Book? Why Now?

This book wasn't written to throw anyone under the bus.
Or to scream for justice.
Or to craft a tidy, triumphant narrative with chapter bows and
moral takeaways.

I wrote this because I had to.

Because there were stories lodged in my lungs
and truths stuck in my thumbs
that wouldn't stop pressing
until they made their way to the page.

Yes—this entire book
was written on my phone.
Every page. Every pause. Every punch to the gut.
Tapped out with my thumbs
on lunch breaks,
between diaper changes and student essays, in waiting rooms,
on sleepless nights and sacred mornings.

In the thick of life that never really slowed down.

So, why this book?
Why now?
Because silence is too expensive.
And staying quiet has cost me enough.

I did it for...

Scout—
My beautiful strong, wildly bright girl.
May the things that happened to me never happen to you.
But if they do—may you know without question:
I will believe you.
I will fight for you.
I will hold you.
No matter what.
You don't have to earn your worth.
You already shine.

My boys—Nickolas and Nathan.
You are not just my sons—
You are the reason I'm still here.
The reason I kept breathing
when it felt impossible.
You held me to this earth
without even knowing it.

Your laughter,
your needs,
your growing-up years—
they tethered me
when I felt unanchored.

They gave me something to rise for.
May you continue to grow into men
who lead with tenderness,
who choose presence over perfection,
and who know that real strength
is found in softness, too.

May you love your wives,
your children,
your people—
but most importantly,
may you never forget
to love yourselves.

You've seen me fall apart.
You've seen me rebuild.
And through it all,
you've made me feel
like I still mattered.

Nicole—
The one who saw me before I saw myself.
Who has loved me through layers I didn't know needed
peeling.

Thank you for your patience.
Your presence.
Your willingness to hold the truth,
even when it was heavy,
even when it wasn't yours to fix.

Thank you for not rushing my healing.
For holding space instead of solutions.

For standing beside me
when I was still figuring out how to stand at all.

You never asked me to be more
than I was ready to be.
You never rushed me
into the light.
You just stood there,
steady and open,
until I remembered how to walk toward it.

You have loved me
in every form—
the broken,
the rebuilding,
the unbecoming,
and the becoming.

You've helped me become
not just the woman I dreamed of being—
but the mother, partner, and truth-teller
I was always capable of becoming.

You've been the evidence
that love doesn't fix you—
it frees you.

I love you more than morning walks,
long talks,
the first sip of coffee on a quiet porch,
and my phone.
And that's saying something.

For the one who smiles through pain—
The one afraid to speak up.
To take up space.
To tell the truth.
I see you.
You're not alone.
You are not too much.
And your story is not too late.

Just remember.
We don't rise alone.
And we sure as hell don't heal in silence.

And for me—
This wasn't just a book.
It was a breaking open.
It was therapy.
It was church.
It was freedom.

This was my way back to myself.
To the voice I lost.
To the girl I buried.
To the woman who finally came home.

I didn't write it for vengeance.
I wrote it for reclamation.
Of my voice.
My story.
My light.

This wasn't just my memoir.
It was my hidden track.

The one you don't expect.
The one that lingers.
The one you sit with
long after the playlist ends.

If just one person reads it
and finally feels seen—
then it's done its job.

Now go.
Write your hidden track.
Say the things.
Sing the truth.
Speak.
Shout.
Whisper.
Roar.
Even if your voice shakes.
Even if it's just for you.

AUTHOR'S NOTE

I didn't write this book because I had it all figured out.

I wrote it because I finally stopped trying to.

These pages were never about perfection—
they were about permission.

To speak.
To feel.
To be seen.

If you found yourself somewhere in these stories—
between the laughter and the ache—
then maybe you've been walking this road too.

And if so, I hope this reminds you:
you are not alone.
You are not behind.
You are becoming.

Every story in here—mine, yours, ours—
is proof that light can live in the cracks.
That healing isn't a straight line.
And that sometimes, coming home to yourself
is the bravest thing you'll ever do.

Here's to the cracks, the courage, and the light that found its
way in,
Nicole

Playlist Disclaimer

The songs referenced in this book are included as part of a personal storytelling experience. All rights to the music, lyrics, and titles mentioned belong to the respective artists, songwriters, and copyright holders. No copyright infringement is intended. This playlist is shared to enhance the emotional landscape of the memoir and is meant for reflective purposes only.

ABOUT THE AUTHOR

If you made it this far, you already know more about me than some people I've known my whole life. I'm Nicole Morrison — writer, coach, educator, and the person who somehow turned a mixtape of memories into a whole book.

I'm equal parts resilience and ridiculous timing, a mother of three wildly different humans, and a wife to the other Nicole... which makes introductions fun and health insurance confusing.

I believe in second chances, honest conversations, and the kind of light that doesn't erase the dark but helps you walk through it with your head up.

When I'm not writing or untangling other people's stories, I'm usually drinking lukewarm coffee, teaching college students how to market and manage businesses (and sometimes their lives), or helping women business owners remember who they were before the world told them otherwise.

I founded Live Differently Publishing because I didn't want to wait for a door to open — so I built my own. If this book made you feel seen, comforted, cracked open, or understood... good. That's why I wrote it.

I live in North Dakota, a place that builds a certain kind of resilience. So does writing a memoir, apparently.

LIVE DIFFERENTLY
PUBLISHING

nmstrategy.com

instagram.com/nicole.morrison2.0
linkedin.com/in/nmstrategy